CHENG & TSUI

"Bringing Asia to the World"™

中文听说读写

INTEGRATED CHINESE

Simplified Characters

1

Workbook

4th Edition

Yuehua Liu and Tao-chung Yao
Nyan-Ping Bi, Yaohua Shi, Liangyan Ge

Original Edition by Tao-chung Yao and Yuehua Liu
Yea-fen Chen, Liangyan Ge, Nyan-Ping Bi, Xiaojun Wang

CHENG & TSUI

"Bringing Asia to the World"™

Publisher
JILL CHENG

Editorial Manager
BEN SHRAGGE

Editors
LEI WANG with LIJIE QIN, MIKE YONG, and
RANDY TELFER

Creative Director
CHRISTIAN SABOGAL

Interior Design
LIZ YATES

Illustrator
KATE PAPADAKI

Cheng & Tsui Company, Inc.
Phone (617) 988-2400 / (800) 554-1963
Fax (617) 426-3669
25 West Street
Boston, MA 02111-1213 USA
chengtsui.co

Contents

Preface   v

Basics   1

Lesson 1: Greetings   11
Dialogue 1: Exchanging Greetings   12
Dialogue 2: Where Are You From?   17

Lesson 2: Family   27
Dialogue 1: Looking at a Family Photo   28
Dialogue 2: Discussing Family   35

Lesson 3: Time and Date   45
Dialogue 1: Out for a Birthday Dinner   46
Dialogue 2: Dinner Invitation   55

Lesson 4: Hobbies   63
Dialogue 1: Discussing Hobbies   64
Dialogue 2: Let's Play Ball   71

Lesson 5: Visiting Friends   81
Dialogue: Visiting a Friend's Place   82
Narrative: At a Friend's Place   91

Bringing It Together (Lessons 1–5)   99

Lesson 6: Making Appointments   103
Dialogue 1: Calling Your Teacher   104
Dialogue 2: Calling a Friend for Help   113

Lesson 7: Studying Chinese   121
Dialogue 1: How Did You Do on the Exam?   122
Dialogue 2: Preparing for Chinese Class   131

Lesson 8: School Life   139
Diary Entry: A Typical School Day   140
Letter: Writing to a Friend   149

Lesson 9: Shopping   159
Dialogue 1: Shopping for Clothes   160
Dialogue 2: Exchanging Shoes   167

Lesson 10: Transportation   177
Dialogue: Going Home for Winter Vacation   178
Email: Thanks for the Ride   185

Bringing It Together (Lessons 6–10)   193

Preface

In designing the workbook exercises for *Integrated Chinese* (IC), we strove to give equal emphasis to the core language skills of listening, speaking, reading, and writing. For the new edition, we have also added *pinyin* and tone exercises for students to progressively improve their pronunciation, extra writing exercises to test their knowledge of Chinese characters, and lesson opener checklists so they can track their learning. Where appropriate, we have labeled the exercises as interpretive, interpersonal, or presentational according to the American Council on the Teaching of Foreign Languages (ACTFL) *21st Century Skills Map for World Languages*.

In addition to the print editions, the IC workbooks are also available online through the ChengTsui Web App (*Essential* and *Educator Editions*). In the digital format, the exercises are presented alongside the textbook content, and feature auto-grading capability. For more information and a free trial, visit chengtsui.co.

Organizational Principles

As with the textbooks, the IC workbooks do not follow one pedagogical methodology, but instead blend several effective teaching approaches. When accessed through the ChengTsui Web App, the workbooks are particularly suited for differentiated instruction, blended learning, and the flipped classroom. Here are some features that distinguish the IC workbooks:

Form and Function
The ultimate purpose of learning any language is to be able to communicate in that language. With that goal in mind, we pay equal attention to language form and function. In addition to traditional workbook exercise types (e.g., fill-in-the-blanks, sentence completion, translation, multiple choice), we include task-based assignments that equip students to handle real-life situations using accurate and appropriate language. These exercises provide linguistic context and are written to reflect idiomatic usage.

Visual Learning
Engaging learners through rich visuals is key to our pedagogy. To build a bridge between the classroom and the target language setting, we include a range of exercises centered on authentic materials. We also include illustration-based exercises that prompt students to answer questions directly in Chinese without going through the process of translation.

Learner-Centered Tasks
We believe that workbook exercises should not only align with the textbook, but also relate to students' lives. We include exercises that simulate daily life and reference culturally relevant topics and themes, including social media and globalization. We hope such open-ended exercises will actively engage students in the subject matter, and keep them interested in the language-learning process.

Differentiated Instruction
We have designed the exercises at different difficulty levels to suit varying curricular needs. Therefore, teachers should assign the exercises at their discretion; they may use some or all of them, in any sequence. Moreover, teachers may complement the workbook exercises with their own materials or with supplementary resources available at chengtsui.co.

Bringing It Together
Every five lessons, we provide a short cumulative review unit ("Bringing It Together") for students who wish to check their progress. These flexible units do not introduce any new learning materials, and can be included in or excluded from curricula according to individual needs.

For maximum flexibility in pacing, each lesson is divided into two parts corresponding to the lesson halves in the textbook. Teachers may spend two or three days teaching the first half and assigning students the associated exercises, then devote an equal amount of time to the second half and its exercises. Teachers may also give two separate vocabulary tests for the two readings to ease student workload.

The workbook lesson sections are as follows:

Listening Comprehension

All too often, listening comprehension is sacrificed in the formal classroom setting. Because of time constraints, students tend to focus their time and energy on mastering a few grammar points. We include a substantial number of listening comprehension exercises to remedy this imbalance. There are two categories of listening exercises; both can be done on students' own time or in the classroom. In either case, the instructor should review students' answers for accuracy.

The first group of listening exercises, which is placed at the beginning of this section, is based on the scenarios in the lesson. For the exercises to be meaningful, students should study the vocabulary list before listening to the recordings.

The second group of listening exercises is based on audio recordings of two or more short dialogues or narratives. These exercises are designed to give students extra practice on the vocabulary and grammar points introduced in the lesson. Some of the exercises, especially those that ask students to choose among several possible answers, are significantly more difficult than others. These exercises should be assigned towards the end of the lesson, after students have familiarized themselves with its content.

Streaming audio for the workbooks (and textbooks) is accessible at chengtsui.co.

Pinyin and Tone

This new section includes exercises that ask students to identify characters with the same initials or finals and write them in *pinyin*; and to indicate the tones of characters that are pronounced similarly. These exercises build on the foundation provided by the Basics section.

Speaking

As with Listening Comprehension, this section includes two groups of exercises. They should be assigned separately based on students' proficiency level.

To help students apply new vocabulary and grammar knowledge to meaningful communication, we first ask questions related to the dialogue or narrative, and then ask questions related to their own lives. These questions require a one- or two-sentence answer. By stringing together short questions and answers, students can construct their own short dialogues, practice in pairs, or take turns asking or answering questions.

As their confidence increases, students can progress to more difficult questions that invite them to express opinions on a number of topics. Typically, these questions are abstract, so they gradually teach students to express their opinions in longer conversations. As the school year progresses, these questions should take up more class discussion time. Because this second group of speaking exercises is quite challenging, it should be attempted only after students are well grounded in the lesson's grammar and vocabulary. Usually, this does not occur immediately after students have completed the first group of exercises.

Reading Comprehension

This section includes questions asking students to match terms, answer questions in English, or answer multiple-choice questions based on readings. There are also activities based on realia.

Writing and Grammar

Characters

These newly added exercises develop students' analytic ability by asking them to apply their knowledge of radicals and patterns. Where appropriate, space to practice writing characters is also provided.

Grammar and Usage

These drills and exercises are designed to solidify students' grasp of important grammar points. Through brief exchanges, students answer questions using specific grammatical forms, or are given sentences to complete. Because they must provide context for these exercises, students cannot treat them as simple mechanical repetition drills.

In the last three lessons, students are introduced to increasingly sophisticated and abstract vocabulary. Corresponding exercises help them to grasp the nuances of new words.

Translation

Translation has been a tool for language teaching through the ages, and positive student feedback confirms our belief in its continued importance. The exercises we have devised serve two primary functions: one, to have students apply specific grammatical structures; and two, to encourage students to build on their vocabulary. Ultimately, we believe this dual-pronged approach will enable students to realize that it takes more than just literal translation to convey an idea in a foreign language.

Writing Practice

This group of exercises is the culmination of the section, as it encourages students to express themselves through writing. Many of the topics overlap with those used in oral practice. We expect that students will find it easier to write what they have already learned to express orally.

Note: Prefaces to the previous editions of IC are available at chengtsui.co.

Basics

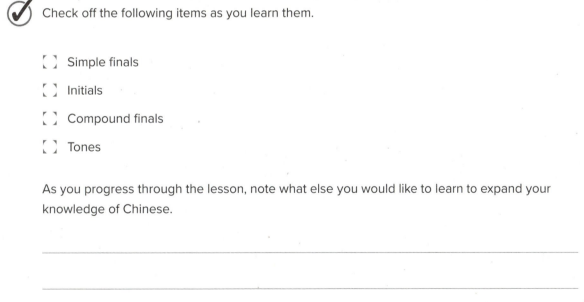

Check off the following items as you learn them.

[ ] Simple finals

[ ] Initials

[ ] Compound finals

[ ] Tones

As you progress through the lesson, note what else you would like to learn to expand your knowledge of Chinese.

_____

_____

_____

Audio

Listen to the audio, then circle the correct answers.

A | **Simple Finals**

1 a. *bā*   b. *bū*   3 a. *gū*   b. *gē*   5 a. *lú*   b. *lǘ*

2 a. *kē*   b. *kā*   4 a. *pū*   b. *pō*

B | **Initials**

1 a. *pà*   b. *bà*   10 a. *kuì*   b. *huì*   19 a. *sè*   b. *shè*

2 a. *pí*   b. *bí*   11 a. *kǎi*   b. *hǎi*   20 a. *sè*   b. *cè*

3 a. *nán*   b. *mán*   12 a. *kuā*   b. *huā*   21 a. *zhǒng*   b. *jiǒng*

4 a. *fú*   b. *hú*   13 a. *jiān*   b. *qiān*   22 a. *shēn*   b. *sēn*

5 a. *tīng* b. *dīng*   14 a. *yú*   b. *qú*   23 a. *rù*   b. *lù*

6 a. *tǒng* b. *dǒng*   15 a. *xiāng* b. *shāng*   24 a. *xiào*   b. *shào*

7 a. *nán*   b. *lán*   16 a. *chú*   b. *rú*   25 a. *qì*   b. *chì*

8 a. *niàn* b. *liàn*   17 a. *zhá*   b. *zá*

9 a. *gàn*   b. *kàn*   18 a. *zì*   b. *cì*

C | **Compound Finals**

1 a. *tuō*   b. *tōu*   10 a. *píng*   b. *pín*   19 a. *téng*   b. *tóng*

2 a. *guǒ*   b. *gǒu*   11 a. *làn*   b. *luàn*   20 a. *kēng*   b. *kōng*

3 a. *duò*   b. *dòu*   12 a. *huán*   b. *hán*   21 a. *pàn*   b. *pàng*

4 a. *diū*   b. *dōu*   13 a. *fēng*   b. *fēn*   22 a. *fǎn*   b. *fǎng*

5 a. *liú*   b. *lóu*   14 a. *bèng*   b. *bèn*   23 a. *mín*   b. *míng*

6 a. *yǒu*   b. *yǔ*   15 a. *lún*   b. *léng*   24 a. *pēn*   b. *pān*

7 a. *nǔ*   b. *nǚ*   16 a. *bīn*   b. *bīng*   25 a. *rén*   b. *rán*

8 a. *lú*   b. *lǘ*   17 a. *kěn*   b. *kǔn*

9 a. *yuán* b. *yán*   18 a. *héng*   b. *hóng*

D | **Tones: First and Fourth (Level and Falling)**

1 a. *bō*   b. *bò*   5 a. *qū*   b. *qù*   9 a. *xià*   b. *xiā*

2 a. *pān* b. *pàn*   6 a. *sì*   b. *sī*   10 a. *yā*   b. *yà*

3 a. *wù*   b. *wū*   7 a. *fēi* b. *fèi*

4 a. *tà*   b. *tā*   8 a. *duì* b. *duī*

E | **Tones: Second and Third (Rising and Low)**

1 a. *mǎi*   b. *mái*   5 a. *wú*   b. *wǔ*   9 a. *féi*   b. *fěi*

2 a. *fǎng* b. *fáng*   6 a. *bǎ*   b. *bá*   10 a. *láo*   b. *lǎo*

3 a. *tú*   b. *tǔ*   7 a. *zhǐ* b. *zhí*

4 a. *gé*   b. *gě*   8 a. *huī* b. *huí*

F　All Four Tones

1　a. *bà*　b. *bā*
2　a. *pí*　b. *pì*
3　a. *méi*　b. *měi*
4　a. *wēn*　b. *wěn*
5　a. *zǎo*　b. *zāo*
6　a. *yōu*　b. *yóu*
7　a. *guāng*　b. *guǎng*
8　a. *cí*　b. *cǐ*
9　a. *qì*　b. *qí*

10　a. *mào*　b. *máo*
11　a. *bǔ*　b. *bù*
12　a. *kuàng*　b. *kuāng*
13　a. *jú*　b. *jǔ*
14　a. *qiáng*　b. *qiāng*
15　a. *xián*　b. *xiān*
16　a. *yǒng*　b. *yòng*
17　a. *zú*　b. *zū*
18　a. *suī*　b. *suí*

19　a. *zhèng*　b. *zhēng*
20　a. *chòu*　b. *chóu*
21　a. *shuāi*　b. *shuài*
22　a. *wǒ*　b. *wò*
23　a. *yào*　b. *yáo*
24　a. *huī*　b. *huì*
25　a. *rú*　b. *rù*

G　Comprehensive Exercise

1　a. *jiā*　b. *zhā*
2　a. *chuí*　b. *qué*
3　a. *chǎng*　b. *qiǎng*
4　a. *xū*　b. *shū*
5　a. *shuǐ*　b. *xuě*
6　a. *zǎo*　b. *zhǎo*
7　a. *zǎo*　b. *cǎo*
8　a. *sōu*　b. *shōu*
9　a. *tōu*　b. *tuō*

10　a. *dǒu*　b. *duǒ*
11　a. *duǒ*　b. *zuǒ*
12　a. *mǎi*　b. *měi*
13　a. *chóu*　b. *qiú*
14　a. *yuè*　b. *yè*
15　a. *jiǔ*　b. *zhǒu*
16　a. *nǔ*　b. *nǚ*
17　a. *zhú*　b. *jú*
18　a. *jī*　b. *zì*

19　a. *liè*　b. *lüè*
20　a. *jīn*　b. *zhēn*
21　a. *xiǔ*　b. *shǒu*
22　a. *kǔn*　b. *hěn*
23　a. *shǎo*　b. *xiǎo*
24　a. *zhǎng*　b. *jiǎng*
25　a. *qū*　b. *chū*

Tone Combination Exercise

Audio

Listen to the words in the audio, then indicate the tones with 1 (first tone), 2 (second tone), 3 (third tone), 4 (fourth tone), or 0 (neutral tone) in the spaces provided. Note that the images in exercise A depict the meaning of the words.

A　Multisyllabic Words

1

_____

2

_____

3

_____

4

_____

5

_____

6

_____

7

9

11

_____

_____

_____

8

10

12

_____

_____

_____

B Disyllabic Words

1 _____

11 _____

21 _____

2 _____

12 _____

22 _____

3 _____

13 _____

23 _____

4 _____

14 _____

24 _____

5 _____

15 _____

25 _____

6 _____

16 _____

26 _____

7 _____

17 _____

27 _____

8 _____

18 _____

28 _____

9 _____

19 _____

29 _____

10 _____

20 _____

30 _____

🔊
Audio

Initials and Simple Finals

Listen to the audio, then fill in the blanks with the appropriate initials or simple finals.

A 1. __a   2. p__   3. __u   4. l__

B 1. f__   2. n__   3. __i   4. __u

C 1. __a   2. l__   3. l__   4. __u

D 1. __u   2. t__   3. n__   4. n__

E 1. __e   2. __u   3. __a

F	1. *g*___	2. *k*___	3. *h*___	
G	1. ___*u*	2. ___*i*	3. ___*u*	
H	1. *j*___	2. *q*___	3. *x*___	
I	1. ___*a*	2. ___*e*	3. ___*i*	4. ___*u*
J	1. ___*u*	2. *c*___	3. ___*u*	4. ___*i*
K	1. ___*i*	2. *s*___	3. ___*a*	4. *q*___
L	1. ___*a*	2. ___*i*	3. *s*___	4. ___*u*
M	1. *c*___	2. ___*i*	3. ___*u*	4. ___*a*
N	1. ___*u*	2. *r*___	3. *ch*___	4. ___*e*

Audio

Tones

Listen to the audio, then add the correct tone marks.

A	1. *he*	2. *ma*	3. *pa*	4. *di*
B	1. *nü*	2. *re*	3. *chi*	4. *zhu*
C	1. *mo*	2. *qu*	3. *ca*	4. *si*
D	1. *tu*	2. *fo*	3. *ze*	4. *ju*
E	1. *lü*	2. *bu*	3. *xi*	4. *shi*
F	1. *gu*	2. *se*	3. *ci*	4. *ku*
G	1. *mang*	2. *quan*	3. *yuan*	4. *yue*
H	1. *yi*	2. *er*	3. *san*	4. *si*
I	1. *ba*	2. *qi*	3. *liu*	4. *wu*
J	1. *jiu*	2. *shi*	3. *tian*	4. *jin*
K	1. *mu*	2. *shui*	3. *huo*	4. *ren*
L	1. *yu*	2. *zhuang*	3. *qun*	4. *zhong*

Compound Finals

Audio

Listen to the audio, then fill in the blanks with the appropriate compound finals.

1	a. *zh*___	b. *t*___	c. *k*___	d. *j*___
2	a. *x*___	b. *q*___	c. *j*___	d. *d*___
3	a. *x*___	b. *zh*___	c. *t*___	d. *g*___
4	a. *sh*___	b. *b*___	c. *z*___	d. *q*___
5	a. *j*___	b. *d*___	c. *x*___	d. *ch*___
6	a. *zh*___	b. *l*___	c. *k*___	d. *j*___
7	a. *s*___	b. *x*___	c. *p*___	d. *ch*___

Audio

Compound Finals and Tones

Listen to the audio, then fill in the blanks with the appropriate compound finals and tone marks.

1 a. *m___*   b. *zh___*   c. *sh___*   d. *zh___*

2 a. *sh___*   b. *t___*   c. *l___*   d. *b___*

3 a. *s___`*   b. *j___*   c. *k___*   d. *d___*

4 a. *l___*   b. *q___*   c. *t___*   d. *x___*

5 a. *f___*   b. *p___*   c. *x___*   d. *j___*

6 a. *b___*   b. *j___*   c. *q___*   d. *t___*

7 a. *l___*   b. *g___*   c. *q___*   d. *x___*

Audio

Neutral Tone

Listen to the words in the audio one at a time, then indicate the tones with 1 (first tone), 2 (second tone), 3 (third tone), 4 (fourth tone), or 0 (neutral tone).

1 _____

8 _____ (older brother)

2 _____

9 _____ (younger brother)

3 _____

10 _____ (older sister)

4 _____

11 _____ (younger sister)

5 _____ (father)

6 _____ (mother)

7 _____ (son)

Initials, Finals, and Tones: Disyllabic Words

Listen to the audio, then circle the correct answers.

1 a. *làoshī*   b. *lǎoshī*   c. *lǎoshí*   (teacher)
2 a. *nǚ'ér*   b. *nǚ'èr*   c. *nǚ'ér*   (daughter)
3 a. *zhàopiàn*   b. *zhāopiàn*   c. *zháopiàn*   (photograph)
4 a. *wǎnfàn*   b. *wǎnfān*   c. *wǎnfàn*   (dinner)
5 a. *shēngrì*   b. *shéngrì*   c. *shěngrì*   (birthday)
6 a. *zāijiàn*   b. *zàijiàn*   c. *záijiàn*   (goodbye)
7 a. *xuéshēng*   b. *xuèsheng*   c. *xuésheng*   (student)
8 a. *diànyǐng*   b. *diānyǐng*   c. *diànyìng*   (movie)
9 a. *zuòtiān*   b. *zuótiān*   c. *zuótiàn*   (yesterday)
10 a. *suírán*   b. *suīrán*   c. *suīràn*   (although)
11 a. *xièxiè*   b. *shèshe*   c. *xièxie*   (thanks)
12 a. *kāfēi*   b. *káfēi*   c. *kāifēi*   (coffee)
13 a. *kělè*   b. *kělè*   c. *kělà*   (cola)
14 a. *píngcháng*   b. *pēngchán*   c. *píngchèng*   (normally)
15 a. *gōngzuò*   b. *gōngzhuò*   c. *gōngzòu*   (work)
16 a. *piàoliàng*   b. *piāoliang*   c. *piàoliang*   (pretty)
17 a. *wèntì*   b. *wèntí*   c. *wěntí*   (questions)
18 a. *rōngyì*   b. *lóngyì*   c. *róngyì*   (easy)
19 a. *kāishǐ*   b. *kāixǐ*   c. *kāisǐ*   (begin)
20 a. *lòudiǎn*   b. *liùdiǎn*   c. *liùdǎn*   (six o'clock)

Initials, Finals, and Tones: Monosyllabic Words

Audio

Listen to the audio, then transcribe what you hear into *pinyin* with tone marks.

1  _____

2  _____

3  _____

4  _____

5  _____

6  _____

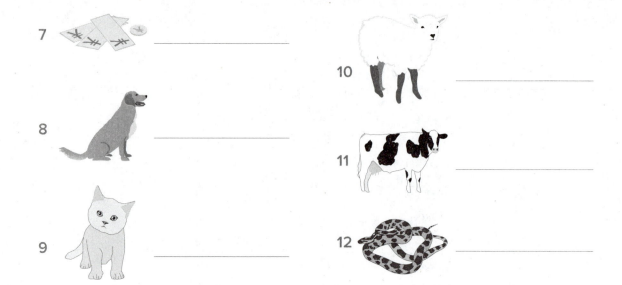

7 _____

8 _____

9 _____

10 _____

11 _____

12 _____

Initials, Finals, and Tones: Cities

Listen to the *pinyin* words in the left column, then connect them with the corresponding cities in the right column, e.g.:

Mài'āmì ⟶ Miami

1 ___ *Bōshìdùn*   a.   Venice

2 ___ *Lúndūn*   b.   Toronto

3 ___ *Niǔyuē*   c.   Boston

4 ___ *Bālí*   d.   Chicago

5 ___ *Zhījiāgē*   e.   Seattle

6 ___ *Běijīng*   f.   New York

7 ___ *Luòshānjī*   g.   Paris

8 ___ *Duōlúnduō*   h.   London

9 ___ *Xīyǎtú*   i.   Beijing

10 ___ *Wēinísī*   j.   Los Angeles

Initials, Finals, and Tones: Countries

Listen to the audio, transcribe what you hear into *pinyin* with tone marks, then identify the countries, e.g.:

Rìběn ⟶ Japan

1 _____ ⟶ _____

2 _____ ⟶ _____

3 _____ $\longrightarrow$ _____

4 _____ $\longrightarrow$ _____

5 _____ $\longrightarrow$ _____

6 _____ $\longrightarrow$ _____

7 _____ $\longrightarrow$ _____

8 _____ $\longrightarrow$ _____

9 _____ $\longrightarrow$ _____

10 _____ $\longrightarrow$ _____

Initials, Finals, and Tones: American Presidents

Audio

Listen to the audio, transcribe what you hear into *pinyin* with tone marks, then identify the American presidents.

1 _____ $\longrightarrow$ _____

2 _____ $\longrightarrow$ _____

3 _____ $\longrightarrow$ _____

4 _____ $\longrightarrow$ _____

5 _____ $\longrightarrow$ _____

6 _____ $\longrightarrow$ _____

7 _____ $\longrightarrow$ _____

8 _____ $\longrightarrow$ _____

9 _____ $\longrightarrow$ _____

10 _____ $\longrightarrow$ _____

The tones for the three characters on the sign are 2, 3, and 4, respectively. Can you pronounce what's on the sign? If you can, then you know how to say "emergency room" in Chinese.

问好
Greetings

 Check off the following items as you learn them.

Useful Expressions

[ ] Hello!

[ ] What's your name?

[ ] My name is _____ (your name).

[ ] I'm a student.

[ ] I'm _____ (your nationality).

Cultural Norms

[ ] Polite introductions

[ ] Standard forms of address

[ ] Common family names

[ ] Proper name order

As you progress through the lesson, note other useful expressions and cultural norms you would like to learn.

_____

_____

_____

Dialogue 1: Exchanging Greetings

Audio

A Listen to the Textbook Dialogue 1 audio, then circle the most appropriate choice. INTERPRETIVE

1 What does the man first say to the woman?
a What's your name?
b I'm Mr. Wang.
c Are you Miss Li?
d How do you do?

2 What is the woman's full name?
a Wang Peng
b Li You
c Xing Li
d Jiao Liyou

3 What is the man's full name?
a Wang Peng
b Li You
c Xing Wang
d Jiao Wangpeng

B Listen to the Workbook Dialogue 1* audio, then circle the most appropriate choice. INTERPRETIVE

1 These two people are
a saying goodbye to each other.
b asking each other's name.
c greeting each other.
d asking each other's nationality.

C Listen to the Workbook Dialogue 2 audio, then circle the most appropriate choice. INTERPRETIVE

1 The two speakers are most likely
a brother and sister.
b father and daughter.
c two old friends being reunited.
d strangers getting acquainted.

2 These two people are
a Mr. Li and Miss You.
b Mr. Li and Miss Li.
c Mr. Wang and Miss You.
d Mr. Wang and Miss Li.

* In Listening Comprehension, references to Workbook Dialogues and Narratives correspond to audio recordings of new Chinese texts, not the dialogues and narratives from the textbook.

A Identify the characters with the same initials (either *x* or *sh*) and write them in *pinyin*.

先　什　姓　小

1　*x:* _____

2　*sh:* _____

B Compare the tones of these characters. Indicate the tones with 1 (first tone), 2 (second tone), 3 (third tone), 4 (fourth tone), or 0 (neutral tone).

1　你 _____　问 _____

2　我 _____　叫 _____

3　什 _____　么 _____

Speaking

A Answer these questions in Chinese based on Textbook Dialogue 1. PRESENTATIONAL

1　How does Mr. Wang greet Miss Li?

2　What is Miss Li's reply?

3　How does Mr. Wang ask what Miss Li's family name is?

4　What is Mr. Wang's given name?

5　How does Mr. Wang ask what Miss Li's given name is?

6　What is Miss Li's given name?

B In pairs, role-play meeting someone for the first time. Try to complete the following tasks in Chinese. INTERPERSONAL

1　Exchange greetings with each other.

2　Ask each other's family name and given name.

A Read these Chinese sentences: 你好，先生。请问你贵姓？ Then mark these statements true or false. INTERPRETIVE

1 _____ The question is addressed to a man.

2 _____ The speaker is talking to his/her friend.

3 _____ The sentence occurs at the end of a conversation.

4 _____ We do not know the addressee's family name.

B Read these Chinese sentences: 小姐，你好。我姓李，叫李朋。你呢？ Then mark these statements true or false. INTERPRETIVE

1 _____ The speaker is talking to a man.

2 _____ We don't know whether the speaker is a man or a woman.

3 _____ We know the speaker's full name.

4 _____ The speaker knows the addressee's full name.

Writing and Grammar

A Which of these characters are based on the left-right pattern, and which on the top-bottom pattern? After filling in the answers, write the characters in the spaces provided.

Left - Right	Top - Bottom
a	b

1 ___ 你

2 ___ 贵

3 ___ 请

4 ___ 什

5 ___ 李

6 ___ 朋

Rearrange these Chinese words into a complete sentence. Use the English in parentheses as a clue. PRESENTATIONAL

1 叫 | 名字 | 你 | 请问 | 什么

(May I ask what your name is?)

_____

2 王朋 | 我 | 叫

(My name is Wang Peng.)

_____

3 姓 | 李 | 我

(My family name is Li.)

_____

C Rewrite and answer these questions in characters. PRESENTATIONAL

1 _Nǐ hǎo!_

_____

2 _Nǐ guì xìng?_

_____

3 _Nǐ jiào shénme míngzi?_

_____

Translate these sentences into Chinese. PRESENTATIONAL

1　Hi, Mr. Wang.

_____

2　**Q:**　May I ask what your family name is?

_____

　　A:　My family name is Li. My name is Li You.

_____

E　Write your Chinese name, if you have one, in characters. If you don't, come up with one (ask your teacher for help if needed).

_____

Dialogue 2: Where Are You From?

Listening Comprehension

A Listen to the Textbook Dialogue 2 audio, then mark these statements true or false. Quote the key sentence from the dialogue, in either *pinyin* or characters, to support your answer. INTERPRETIVE

1 _____ Miss Li is a student.

_____

2 _____ Mr. Wang is a teacher.

_____

3 _____ Mr. Wang is American.

_____

4 _____ Miss Li is Chinese.

_____

B Listen to the Workbook Dialogue 1 audio, then mark these statements true or false. INTERPRETIVE

1 _____ Both the man and the woman are Chinese.

2 _____ Both the man and the woman are American.

3 _____ The man is Chinese and the woman is American.

4 _____ The man is American and the woman is Chinese.

C Listen to the Workbook Dialogue 2 audio, then mark these statements true or false. INTERPRETIVE

1 _____ Both the man and the woman are teachers.

2 _____ Both the man and the woman are students.

3 _____ The man is a teacher. The woman is a student.

4 _____ The man is a student. The woman is a teacher.

A Identify the characters with the same initials (either *x* or *sh*) and write them in *pinyin*.

先　师　什　姓　是　小

1　*x:* _____

2　*sh:* _____

B Compare the tones of these characters. Indicate the tones with 1 (first tone), 2 (second tone), 3 (third tone), 4 (fourth tone), or 0 (neutral tone).

1　是 _____ 师 _____

Speaking

A Answer these questions in Chinese based on Textbook Dialogue 2. PRESENTATIONAL

1　How does Miss Li ask whether Mr. Wang is a teacher or not?

2　Is Mr. Wang a teacher?

3　Is Miss Li a teacher?

4　What is Mr. Wang's nationality?

5　What is Miss Li's nationality?

B You meet a Chinese person on campus. Ask politely in Chinese whether he/she is a teacher. INTERPERSONAL

C You've just met a foreign student who can speak Chinese. INTERPERSONAL

1　Ask whether he/she is Chinese.

2　Tell him/her that you are American.

D Introduce yourself in Chinese to your class. Tell your classmates what your Chinese name is and whether you are a student. PRESENTATIONAL

A Match the sentences in the left column with the appropriate responses in the right column.
INTERPRETIVE

1 _____ 你好！   a 是，我是老师。

2 _____ 您贵姓？   b 不，我是中国人。

3 _____ 你是美国人吗？   c 我也是学生。

4 _____ 你是老师吗？   d 我姓李。

5 _____ 我是学生，你呢？   e 你好！

B After reading this passage, fill in the chart, then answer the questions that follow by circling the most appropriate choice. INTERPRETIVE

王先生叫王师中。王师中是纽约人，不是中国人。王师中是学生，不是老师。李小姐是北京人，叫李美生。李美生是老师，不是学生。

	Gender	Given Name	Nationality	Occupation	Hometown
王先生					
李小姐					

1 If you were the man's close friend, how would you normally address him?

a Wang Xiansheng

b Xiansheng Wang

c Wang

d Shizhong

2 If you were introduced to the woman for the first time, with which term would it be most appropriate to address her?

a   Li Xiaojie

b   Xiaojie Li

c   Li Meisheng

d   Meisheng

C   Read this dialogue, then answer the questions in English. INTERPRETIVE

李先生：请问，你是王老师吗？

王小姐：是，我是。你是……

李先生：王老师，你好。我姓李，叫李大中。

王小姐：李大中，李大中……ò, 李老师，是你 ya ……你好，你好。

1   Is this a dialogue between a teacher and a student?

_____

2   Are the two speakers very familiar with each other?

_____

3   What tone of voice does the interjection "ò" bring to the dialogue?

_____

4   What tone of voice does the particle "ya" bring to the dialogue?

_____

D   On these three Chinese business cards, underline the characters that are family names. INTERPRETIVE

美国夏威夷大学东亚语文系教授

李 英 哲
YINGCHE LI

EAST ASIAN LANGUAGES AND LITERATURES
UNIVERSITY OF HAWAII
HONOLULU, HAWAII 96822
U.S.A

TEL: (808) 956-xxxx(0)
FAX: (808) 956-xxxx

中外合资
常州华润装饰工程有限公司
CHANGZHOU HUA RUN DECORATION ENGINEERING CO. LTD

王 德 中
WANG DE ZHONG
董事 副总经理

地址：中国常州劳动中路42号
ADD: NO42 LAO DONG RD(M) CHANGZHOU
电话 TEL: 882xxxx 881xxxx
传真 FAX: 0519–882xxxx
电挂 CABLE: 5000 邮编 P.C:213001
宅电 HOME:662xxxx

台北美国学校
外语系中文部主任

王 智 宁

校址：台北市士林区中山北路巷六段八〇〇号
电话：八七三—x x x x 转二四〇
传真：八七三—x x x x x
住宅：台北市中山北路七段114巷57号三楼
电话：/ 传真：（〇二）八七—x x x x x

E Review these two Chinese business cards, then answer the questions in English. INTERPRETIVE

外语教学与研究出版社
北京外语音像出版社

王 伟
音像中心

地址：北京市西三环北路19号（北京外国语大学）
电话：(010)6891 XXXX
手机：13671 XXXX   邮编：100089

美国在台协会华语学校

王 俊 仁

台北市阳明山山仔后   电话：(02) 2861- XXXX
爱富三街长生巷5号   传真：(02) 2861- XXXX

1 What are the card owners' family names?

_____

2 Which business card's owner works in Beijing?

_____

A Which of these characters are based on the unitary pattern, and which on the enclosing pattern? After filling in the answers, write the characters in the spaces provided.

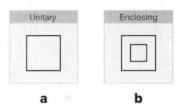

	Unitary	Enclosing
	a	**b**

1 ___ 人

2 ___ 国

3 ___ 中

B Rewrite these sentences in characters. PRESENTATIONAL

1 *Qǐng wèn, nǐ shì xuésheng ma?*

_____

2 *Wǒ shì Zhōngguó rén. Nǐ ne?*

_____

3 *Wǒ bú xìng Wáng, wǒ xìng Lǐ.*

_____

4 *Nǐ shì lǎoshī, wǒ shì xuésheng.*

_____

5 *Nǐ shì Měiguó rén, wǒ yě shì Měiguó rén.*

_____

C Rearrange these Chinese words into sentences, using the English in parentheses as clues. PRESENTATIONAL

1 姓｜王｜吗｜你

(Is your family name Wang?)

_____

2 吗 | 是 | 你 | 学生 | 中国

(Are you a Chinese student?)

_____

3 北京 | 是 | 人 | 我 | 不

(I am not from Beijing.)

_____

4 小姐 | 先生 | 纽约人 | 纽约人 | 王 | 李 |

也 | 是 | 是

(Miss Wang is a New Yorker. Mr. Li is also from New York.)

_____

D Answer these questions in Chinese according to your own circumstances. INTERPERSONAL

1 Q: 你是学生吗？

A: _____

2 Q: 你是北京人吗？

A: _____

3 Q: 李小姐是美国人。你呢？

A: _____

4 Q: 王先生是中国学生。你呢？

A: _____

E Write out the questions to which these statements are the appropriate answers, following the example below. PRESENTATIONAL

我是学生。

你是学生吗？

1 我是美国人。 _____

2 我姓李。 _____

3 王老师是北京人。 _____

4 李小姐不是老师。 _____

5 我也是学生。 _____

李友是学生。| 王朋是学生。

李友是学生，王朋也是学生。

1 你是美国人。| 我是美国人。

_____

2 李小姐不是中国人。| 李先生不是中国人。

_____

3 你不姓王。| 我不姓王。

_____

4 王先生不是纽约人。| 李小姐不是纽约人。

_____

G Complete this conversation in characters based on the information given. PRESENTATIONAL

Student A: _____ 。

Student B: _____ 。

Student A: _____ , _____ ?

Student B: 我姓王。

Student A: _____ ?

Student B: 我叫王京。

Student A: _____, _____?

Student B: 不，我不是，我是中国人。

Student A: _____, _____?

Student B: 我也是。

H Translate these sentences into Chinese. PRESENTATIONAL

1 **Q:** Is Mr. Wang Chinese?

_____

A: Yes, Mr. Wang is from Beijing.

_____

2 **Q:** Li You is a student. How about you?

_____

A: I am also a student.

_____

3 **Q:** I am from New York. Are you from New York, too?

_____

A: No, I am from Beijing.

_____

4 **Q:** My family name is Wang. Is your family name Wang also?

_____

A: No, my family name is not Wang. My family name is Li.

_____

I Write a self-introduction in Chinese by filling in the blanks. PRESENTATIONAL

你好！我姓_____，叫_____。
我是_____人，不是_____人。
我是_____，不是_____。

家庭

Family

 Check off the following items as you learn them.

Useful Expressions

- [ ] There are _____ (number) people in my family.
- [ ] Who is this girl/boy?
- [ ] He/she is my older brother/sister.
- [ ] I don't have any brothers/sisters.
- [ ] My dad/mom is a _____ (profession).

Cultural Norms

- [ ] Kinship terms
- [ ] Family structure
- [ ] Business card etiquette

As you progress through the lesson, note other useful expressions and cultural norms you would like to learn.

_____

_____

_____

Dialogue 1: Looking at a Family Photo

Audio

Listening Comprehension

A Listen to the Textbook Dialogue 1 audio, then mark these statements true or false. INTERPRETIVE

1. _____ Wang Peng knows the people in the picture.

2. _____ Gao Wenzhong doesn't have any older sisters.

3. _____ Gao Wenzhong's parents are in the picture.

4. _____ Gao Wenzhong's younger brother is also in the picture.

5. _____ Gao Wenzhong's older brother doesn't have any daughters.

B Listen to the Workbook Dialogue 1 audio, then circle the most appropriate choice. INTERPRETIVE

1. Who are the people in the picture?

   a. The woman's mother and younger sister.

   b. The woman's mother and older sister.

   c. The woman's older sister and younger sister.

   d. The woman's mother and her mother's sister.

C Listen to the Workbook Dialogue 2 audio, then circle the most appropriate choice. INTERPRETIVE

1. Which of the following statements is true?

   a. Wang Jing is the woman's sister.

   b. Wang Jing is the man's daughter.

   c. Wang Jing is not related to Mr. Wang.

   d. Wang Jing is not related to the woman.

Pinyin and Tone

A Identify the characters with the same initials (either *j* or *zh*) and write them in *pinyin*.

姐　中　照　京　这

1　*j:* _____

2　*zh:* _____

B Compare the tones of these characters. Indicate the tones with 1 (first tone), 2 (second tone), 3 (third tone), 4 (fourth tone), or 0 (neutral tone).

1　他 _____　她 _____

2　问 _____　文 _____

3　哥 _____　个 _____

Speaking

A Answer these questions in Chinese based on Textbook Dialogue 1. PRESENTATIONAL

1　Whose photo is on the wall?

2　Who is the young lady in the picture?

3　Who is the boy in the picture?

4　Does Gao Wenzhong's older brother have a son or a daughter?

B Using a picture found online, introduce your favorite cartoon or celebrity family to a partner. Then ask your partner if there are any older sisters or younger brothers in the family. INTERPERSONAL

Reading Comprehension

A Match these Chinese words with their English equivalents. INTERPRETIVE

1 _____ 爸爸   a mother

2 _____ 大哥   b boy

3 _____ 弟弟   c older sister

4 _____ 女儿   d eldest/oldest brother

5 _____ 妈妈   e younger brother

6 _____ 姐姐   f son

7 _____ 儿子   g girl

8 _____ 男孩子   h father

9 _____ 女孩子   i daughter

B Match the questions on the left with the appropriate replies on the right. INTERPRETIVE

1 _____ 这个人是谁？   a 我没有弟弟。

2 _____ 这是你的照片吗？   b 这是我爸爸。

3 _____ 这个男孩子是你弟弟吗？   c 他有儿子，没有女儿。

4 _____ 你妹妹是学生吗？   d 不是，他是王老师的儿子。

5 _____ 李先生有女儿吗？   e 是我的。

6 _____ 你有弟弟吗？   f 她是学生。

C Read this dialogue, then circle the most appropriate choice. INTERPRETIVE

王朋：李友，这个女孩子是你吗？

李友：不，她是我妈妈。

王朋：你妈妈？这个男孩子是你爸爸吗？

李友：不是，他是我妈妈的大哥。

1 What are the speakers doing while talking?

   a looking at a picture of Wang Peng

   b looking at a picture taken many years ago

   c looking at a picture they took yesterday

   d looking at Li You's parent's picture

2 Who is in the picture?

   a Wang Peng and Li You

   b Li You and her mother

   c Wang Peng and Li You's mother

   d Li You's mother and Li You's uncle

Writing and Grammar

A Which of these characters are based on the left-right pattern, and which on the unitary pattern? After filling in the answers, write the characters in the spaces provided.

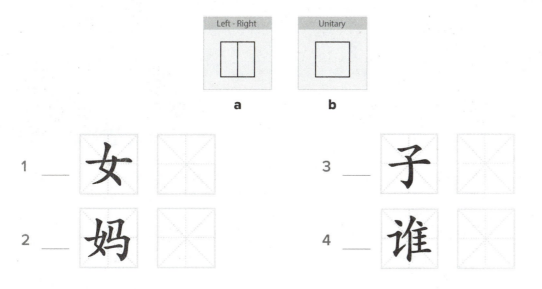

Left - Right   Unitary

       a   b

1 ___ 女

2 ___ 妈

3 ___ 子

4 ___ 谁

5 ___

7 ___

6 ___

B Fill in the blanks with 这 or 那 based on the prompt.

1 You point to a person standing about thirty feet away, and say:

_____ 个人是我的老师，他是北京人。

2 You are holding a family photo in your hand, and say:

_____ 是我爸爸，_____ 是我妈妈。

3 You look down the hallway and recognize someone, and say:

_____ 个人叫李生，是李友的爸爸。

4 You introduce to your friend a girl sitting at the same table, and say:

_____ 是李先生的女儿，李小约。

C Answer these questions based on the image. INTERPERSONAL

1 这个人是谁？／他是谁？

_____

2 这个人是中国人吗？／

他是中国人吗？

_____

D Answer these questions in Chinese according to your own circumstances. INTERPERSONAL

1 你有姐姐吗？

_____

2 你有弟弟吗？

_____

3 你爸爸叫什么名字？

_____

4 你妈妈是老师吗？

_____

E Focus on the underlined words, and write out the questions to which these statements are the appropriate answers. Follow the example below. PRESENTATIONAL

<u>他</u>是王朋。

<u>谁</u>是王朋？

1 这是<u>王老师的</u>照片。

_____

2 那个男孩子是<u>王朋</u>。

_____

F Translate these sentences into Chinese. PRESENTATIONAL

1 **Q:** Little Wang, is this your photograph?

_____

A: This is not my photograph.

_____

2 Q: Mr. Wang doesn't have any sons. How about Mr. Li?

_____

   A: He doesn't, either.

_____

3 Q: Who is this young lady?

_____

   A: She's my older sister.

_____

4 Q: Does your oldest brother have a son?

_____

   A: No, he doesn't have any sons, nor does he have any daughters.

_____

G | Write a summary of a well-known family, including names of family members and their relationships to each other. PRESENTATIONAL

_____

_____

_____

_____

Dialogue 2: Discussing Family

> ## Listening Comprehension

A   Listen to the Textbook Dialogue 2 audio, then circle the most appropriate choice. INTERPRETIVE

1   How many people are there in Bai Ying'ai's family?

    a   three

    b   four

    c   five

    d   six

2   How many people are there in Li You's family?

    a   three

    b   four

    c   five

    d   six

3   How many younger sisters does Bai Ying'ai have?

    a   none

    b   one

    c   two

    d   three

4   How many older sisters does Li You have?

    a   none

    b   one

    c   two

    d   three

5   How many older brothers does Bai Ying'ai have?

    a   none

    b   one

    c   two

    d   three

6   How many younger brothers does Bai Ying'ai have?

    a   none

    b   one

    c   two

    d   three

7   How many children do Bai Ying'ai's parents have?

    a   two

    b   three

    c   four

    d   five

8 How many sons do Li You's parents have?

    a   none

    b   one

    c   two

    d   three

9 What is Bai Ying'ai's father's occupation?

    a   lawyer

    b   teacher

    c   doctor

    d   student

10 What is Li You's mother's occupation?

    a   lawyer

    b   teacher

    c   doctor

    d   student

B Listen to the Workbook Dialogue 1 audio, then circle the most appropriate choice. INTERPRETIVE

1 Which of the following is true?

    a   Both the man and the woman have older brothers.

    b   Both the man and the woman have younger brothers.

    c   The man has an older brother but no younger brothers.

    d   The man has a younger brother but no older brothers.

2 The woman laughs at the end of the conversation because

    a   neither the man nor she herself has any younger brothers.

    b   neither the man nor she herself has any older brothers.

    c   the man failed to count himself as his older brother's younger brother.

    d   the man failed to count himself as his younger brother's older brother.

C Listen to the Workbook Dialogue 2 audio, then circle the most appropriate choice. INTERPRETIVE

1 What is the occupation of the man's mother?

    a   teacher

    b   student

    c   doctor

    d   lawyer

2 What is the occupation of the woman's father?

    a   teacher

    b   student

    c   doctor

    d   lawyer

Listen to the Workbook Dialogue 3 audio, then circle the most appropriate choice. INTERPRETIVE

1 How many brothers does the woman have?

a   one

b   two

c   three

d   four

2 How many daughters do the woman's parents have?

a   one

b   two

c   three

d   four

3 How many people in the woman's family are older than herself?

a   two

b   three

c   four

d   five

4 How many people in the man's family are younger than himself?

a   none

b   one

c   two

d   three

5 When talking about the number of people in his family, the man forgot to include

a   his older brother.

b   his younger sister.

c   his younger brother.

d   himself.

Pinyin and Tone

A   Identify the characters with the same finals (either *uo* or *ou*) and write them in *pinyin*.

口　国　都　有　我

1 *uo:* _____

2 *ou:* _____

Compare the tones of these characters. Indicate the tones with 1 (first tone), 2 (second tone), 3 (third tone), 4 (fourth tone), or 0 (neutral tone).

1 妹 _____ 没 _____

2 做 _____ 作 _____

Speaking

A Answer these questions in Chinese based on Textbook Dialogue 2. PRESENTATIONAL

1 How many people are there in Bai Ying'ai's family?

2 How many brothers and sisters does Li You have?

3 What is Bai Ying'ai's father's occupation?

4 What are Bai Ying'ai's mother's and Li You's mother's occupations?

5 How many people are there in Li You's family?

B Using a family portrait, introduce your family members to the class. PRESENTATIONAL

C In pairs, share family portraits and ask questions about the identity and occupations of family members. INTERPERSONAL

Reading Comprehension

A Mr. Wang and Mr. Li are neighbors. Read this passage about their families, then answer the questions. INTERPRETIVE

王先生是学生。他爸爸是律师，妈妈是英文老师。王先生的哥哥是医生。李先生和他妹妹都是学生。李先生的爸爸和姐姐都是医生，妈妈是老师。

1 If the two families vacation together, how many plane tickets should they book?

_____

2 How many doctors are there between the two families? Who are they?

_____

3 If Mr. Wang's mother were to have a colleague in the Li family, who would it most likely be?

_____

4 How many students are there between the two families?

_____

5 What does Mr. Li's father do? Is anyone from the Wang family in the same profession?

_____

B Read this dialogue, check the proper spaces on the form to indicate the professions of Little Gao's family members, then mark the statements true or false. INTERPRETIVE

小王：请问，你爸爸是律师吗？

小高：不，他是老师。我家有两个老师，两个医生，一个律师。

小王：你家有五口人吗？

小高：不，我家有四口人。我和我妈妈都是医生。我哥哥是老师，也是律师。

	Little Gao	Father	Mother	Older Brother
Lawyer				
Doctor				
Teacher				

1 ____ Little Wang seems to know Little Gao's family very well.

2 ____ Little Gao seems to have miscounted the people in his family.

3 ____ Little Gao's older brother is not only a teacher, but also a lawyer.

C Review this business card, then mark the statements true or false. INTERPRETIVE

韩 沐 新 律师 合伙人

律师事务所

地址： 北京建国门外大街XX号赛特大厦XXXX室　　　邮编： 100004
电话： (8610) 6515 XXXX　　　　　　　直线： (8610)6515 XXXX
手机： 1390115 XXXX　　　　　　　　传真： (8610)6528 XXXX
E-mail: muxinh@ XXXX

1 ____ This person's family name is Li.

2 ____ This person is a doctor.

3 ____ This person works in Beijing.

Writing and Grammar

A Write the characters that include the radical for woman, 女, then provide each character's meaning in English.

爸　妈　哥　弟　姐　妹　他　她

1 _____

2 _____

3 _____

4 _____

B Answer these questions about family in complete sentences, using 有 or 没有.
If your answer is affirmative, state how many siblings you have, following the example
below. INTERPERSONAL

  Q: 你有哥哥吗？

  A: 我有两个哥哥。 (affirmative)

  A: 我没有哥哥。 (negative)

1 Q: 你有哥哥吗？

  A: _____

2 Q: 你有姐姐吗？

  A: _____

3 Q: 你有弟弟吗？

  A: _____

4 Q: 你有妹妹吗？

  A: _____

C Rewrite these sentences using 都, following the example below. PRESENTATIONAL

  小高是学生，王朋也是学生。

  小高和王朋都是学生。

1 高文中有姐姐，李友也有姐姐。

  _____

2 那个男孩子姓李，那个女孩子也姓李。

  _____

3 李友没有我的照片，王朋也没有我的照片。

_____

4 她哥哥不是律师，她弟弟也不是律师。

_____

5 这个人不叫白英爱，那个人也不叫白英爱。

_____

D Fill in the blanks with the appropriate question words: 什么, 谁, 谁的, or 几. PRESENTATIONAL

1 Q: 他妹妹叫_____名字？

A: 他妹妹叫高美美。

2 Q: 李老师家有_____口人？

A: 他家有三口人。

3 Q: 他爸爸做_____工作？

A: 他爸爸是医生。

4 Q: 那个美国人是_____？

A: 他叫 Sam Freedman，是我的老师。

5 Q: 那是_____照片？

A: 那是白律师的照片。

Translate these sentences into Chinese. PRESENTATIONAL

1 Student A: How many people are there in Mr. Wang's family?

_____

   Student B: There are five people in his family.

_____

2 Student A: What do his parents do?

_____

   Student B: Both his mother and father are teachers.

_____

3 Student A: How many daughters does he have?

_____

   Student B: He doesn't have any. He has three boys.

_____

4 Student A: My dad is a doctor. My mom is a lawyer. How about your mom and dad?

_____

   Student B: My mom is a lawyer, too. My dad is a teacher.

_____

5 (Students A and B are looking at a picture on Student B's desk.)

   Student A: Who is this?

_____

   Student B: This is my older sister. Her name is Wang Xiaoying.

_____

   Student A: What does she do?

_____

   Student B: My sister and I both are college students. How many sisters do you have?

_____

   Student A: I have an older sister, too. Here is a picture of her. She has a daughter.

_____

Write about your family. PRESENTATIONAL

1 List your family members in Chinese.

_____

_____

2 State what each of your family members does. It's okay to write their occupations in *pinyin*.

_____

_____

_____

3 Prepare an oral presentation: Write a brief introduction of your family using the framework provided. Memorize the introduction and present your family to the class using a family portrait.

你好，我姓_____，叫_____。
我是____学生。我家有____口人，_____
_____和我。这是我家人的照片。这是我爸
爸，这是我妈妈，这个人是我_____……我
爸爸是_____，妈妈是_____，_____
是_____……

时 间
Time and Date

 Check off the following items as you learn them.

Useful Expressions

[ ] When is your birthday?

[ ] I'll treat you to dinner.

[ ] Thank you very much!

[ ] What time is it now?

[ ] Goodbye!

Cultural Norms

[ ] Date formats

[ ] Calendar types

[ ] Birthday customs

[ ] Counting age

[ ] Auspicious numbers

As you progress through the lesson, note other useful expressions and cultural norms you would like to learn.

_____

_____

_____

Dialogue 1: Out for a Birthday Dinner

Audio

Listening Comprehension

A Listen to the Textbook Dialogue 1 audio, then mark these statements true or false. INTERPRETIVE

1 _____ Gao Wenzhong is eighteen years old this year.

2 _____ September 12 is Thursday.

3 _____ Bai Ying'ai will treat Gao Wenzhong to dinner on Thursday.

4 _____ Gao Wenzhong is American, but he likes Chinese food.

5 _____ Bai Ying'ai refuses to eat Chinese food.

6 _____ They will have dinner together at 6:30 p.m.

B Listen to the Workbook Dialogue 1 audio, then circle the most appropriate choice. INTERPRETIVE

1 What is today's date?
   a May 10
   b June 10
   c October 5
   d October 6

2 What day of the week is it today?
   a Thursday
   b Friday
   c Saturday
   d Sunday

3 What day of the week is October 7?
   a Thursday
   b Friday
   c Saturday
   d Sunday

C Listen to the Workbook Dialogue 2 audio, then circle the most appropriate choice. INTERPRETIVE

1 What time does the man propose to meet for the appointment?
   a 6:30
   b 7:00
   c 7:30
   d 8:00

2 What time do they finally agree upon?

    a   6:30

    b   7:00

    c   7:30

    d   8:00

3 On what day of the week are they going to meet?

    a   Thursday

    b   Friday

    c   Saturday

    d   Sunday

Pinyin and Tone

A   Identify the characters with the same initials (*sh*, *s*, or *x*) and write them in *pinyin*.

岁　十　谢　谁　四　喜

1   *sh:* _____

2   *s:* _____

3   *x:* _____

B   Compare the tones of these characters. Indicate the tones with 1 (first tone), 2 (second tone), 3 (third tone), 4 (fourth tone), or 0 (neutral tone).

1   号 _____   好 _____

2   星 _____   姓 _____

3   还 _____   孩 _____

4   是 _____   十 _____

A Answer these questions in Chinese based on Textbook Dialogue 1. PRESENTATIONAL

1 When is Gao Wenzhong's birthday?

2 How old is Gao Wenzhong?

3 Who is going to treat whom?

4 What is Gao Wenzhong's nationality?

5 What kind of food are they going to have?

6 What time is the dinner?

B In pairs, role-play the following situation. Today is your partner's birthday. Find out how old he/she is and offer to take him/her out to dinner. Ask if he/she prefers Chinese or American food and decide when to eat. INTERPERSONAL

Reading Comprehension

A Based on the information on the sticky note, circle the most appropriate choice. INTERPRETIVE

1 What day of the week is September 15?

  a Monday

  b Tuesday

  c Friday

  d Sunday

2 What is the date of the following Thursday?

  a September 22

  b September 23

  c September 24

  d September 25

B Fill in the blanks in English based on the calendar. INTERPRETIVE

1 The date on this calendar is _____.

2 The day of the week is _____.

3 Next month is _____.

4 The day after tomorrow is a _____.

C Circle the correct way to write "June 3, 2019" in Chinese. INTERPRETIVE

1 6月3号2019年

2 3号6月2019年

3 6月2019年3号

4 2019年6月3号

D Read this passage, then mark the statements true or false. INTERPRETIVE

这个星期六是十一月二号，是小王的妈妈的生日。小王请他妈妈吃饭。王妈妈很喜欢我，小王也请我吃饭。吃什么呢？王妈妈是北京人，喜欢吃中国菜。我是纽约人，可是我也喜欢吃中国菜。

1 _____ Saturday is Little Wang's birthday.

2 _____ Little Wang's mother will take her son to dinner this Saturday.

3 _____ The speaker seems to know Little Wang's mother well.

4 _____ The speaker is American, and Little Wang's mother is Chinese.

5 _____ They will most likely have a Chinese dinner on Saturday.

E What are the dates for the exhibition advertised on this flyer, and on which university campus is it being held? INTERPRETIVE

吉金铸国史
周原出土铜器精粹展

时间：五月四日至八月三十日 AM 9:00 - PM 4:30
展出地点：纽英大学考古与艺术博物馆

A Which of these characters are based on the left-right pattern and which on the top-bottom pattern? After filling in the answers, write the characters in the spaces provided.

a   b

1 ___ 欢   5 ___ 美

2 ___ 英   6 ___ 谁

3 ___ 期   7 ___ 哥

4 ___ 饭

B Write these numbers in Chinese characters. PRESENTATIONAL

1 15 _____

2 93 _____

3 47 _____

4 62 _____

5 Your phone number _____

6 Your birthday _____ 月_____ 号

C Write out the questions to which these statements are the appropriate answers. Use 还是 in each question, following the example below. PRESENTATIONAL

王朋

Q: 王朋是中国人还是美国人?

A: 王朋是中国人。

1 你

Q: _____?

A: 我喜欢吃美国菜。

2 李友的爸爸

Q: _____?

A: 他是律师。

3 高文中

Q: _____?

A: 高文中有姐姐。

D Rearrange these Chinese words into sentences, using the English sentences as clues. PRESENTATIONAL

1 我 | 晚饭 | 你 | 怎么样 | 吃 | 请 | 星期四

(I'll take you out to dinner on Thursday. How about it?)

_____

2 星期四 | 星期五 | 晚饭 | 我 | 你 | 还是 | 请 | 吃

(Are you taking me out to dinner on Thursday or Friday?)

_____

3 哥哥 | 小白 | 喜欢 | 他 | 我 | 我 | 可是 |
不 | 喜欢

(I do not like Little Bai, but I like his older brother.)

_____

4 美国人 | 美国菜 | 可是 | 他 | 不 | 喜欢 |
吃 | 是

(He is American, but he does not like eating American food.)

_____

E Answer these questions according to your own circumstances. INTERPERSONAL

1 Q: 你今年多大?

A: _____

2 Q: 你的生日（是）几月几号?

A: _____

3 Q: 你喜欢吃美国菜还是中国菜?

A: _____

F Translate these sentences into Chinese. PRESENTATIONAL

1 Student A: When is your birthday?

_____

Student B: My birthday is September 30.

_____

2 Student A: What day of the week is September 30?

_____

Student B: September 30 is Friday.

_____

3 Student A: How old are you?

_____

Student B: I'm eighteen.

_____

4 Student A: How about I treat you to dinner on Thursday?

_____

Student B: Great! Thanks. See you Thursday.

_____

5 (Little Wang's girlfriend has never met Little Wang's parents. She is planning to invite them out to dinner, but wants to find out what they like to eat first.)

Little Wang: What time are we having dinner on Saturday night?

_____

Girlfriend: How about 7:30?

_____

Little Wang: Okay. Who are we inviting for dinner?

_____

Girlfriend: We'll invite your mom and dad.

_____

Little Wang: Great.

_____

Girlfriend: Do they like American or Chinese food?

_____

Little Wang: They like American, and they like Chinese, too.

_____

G Complete these tasks in Chinese. PRESENTATIONAL

1 Write down today's date.

_____

2 Write down the current time.

_____

3 Who's your idol/hero? Your idol/hero could be one of your family members or someone famous. If your idol/hero is someone famous, go online and find out his/her age, birthday, family members, and what cuisine he/she prefers. Write a personal profile of your idol/hero, and share it with your teacher/class.

_____

_____

_____

_____

_____

_____

Dialogue 2: Dinner Invitation

Listening Comprehension

A | Listen to the Textbook Dialogue 2 audio, then mark these statements true or false. INTERPRETIVE

1 _____ Wang Peng is not busy today.

2 _____ Wang Peng will be busy tomorrow.

3 _____ Bai Ying'ai is inviting Wang Peng to dinner.

4 _____ Tomorrow is Bai Ying'ai's birthday.

5 _____ Li You is Bai Ying'ai's schoolmate.

B | Listen to the Workbook Dialogue 1 audio, then mark these statements true or false. INTERPRETIVE

1 _____ Both speakers in the dialogue are Chinese.

2 _____ The man invites the woman to dinner because it will be his birthday tomorrow.

3 _____ The man likes Chinese food.

4 _____ The woman only likes American food.

C | Listen to the Workbook Dialogue 2 audio, then mark these statements true or false. INTERPRETIVE

1 _____ Today the woman is busy.

2 _____ Today the man is not busy.

3 _____ Tomorrow both the man and the woman will be busy.

Pinyin and Tone

A | Identify the characters with the same initials (either *j* or *x*) and write them in *pinyin*.

现 京 星 喜 见

1 *j:* _____

2 *x:* _____

B Compare the tones of these characters. Indicate the tones with 1 (first tone), 2 (second tone), 3 (third tone), 4 (fourth tone), or 0 (neutral tone).

1 事 _____ 十 _____

2 人 _____ 认 _____

3 有 _____ 友 _____

Speaking

A Answer these questions in Chinese based on Textbook Dialogue 2. PRESENTATIONAL

1 Why does Bai Ying'ai ask if Wang Peng is busy tomorrow?

2 When is Wang Peng busy?

3 Who else will go to the dinner tomorrow?

4 Does Bai Ying'ai know Li You? How do you know?

B In pairs, ask for today's date, the day of the week, and the current time. INTERPERSONAL

C In pairs, role-play the following scenario. Your partner's sibling has a birthday coming up, and you would like to invite him/her to dinner. Find out when the sibling's birthday is, when he/she is available, and what type of cuisine he/she prefers. INTERPERSONAL

Reading Comprehension

A Rewrite these times in ordinary numeric notation (e.g., 1:00, 2:15, 3:30 p.m.). INTERPRETIVE

1 三点 _____

2 六点三刻 _____

3 晚上八点 _____

4 晚上九点一刻 _____

5 晚上十一点半 _____

Read this dialogue, then mark the statements true or false. **INTERPRETIVE**

男： 你好。今天我请你吃晚饭，怎么样？

女： 是吗？我不认识你，你为什么请我吃饭？

男： 因为今天是我的生日，可是没有人请我吃饭……

女： 先生，你为什么不请你的朋友吃饭？

男： 因为他们今天都很忙。

1 ____ The two people are friends.

2 ____ The man needs someone to celebrate his birthday with him.

3 ____ The woman accepts the man's invitation readily.

4 ____ The woman is the only one that the man invites to dinner.

5 ____ According to the man, his friends are too busy today to celebrate his birthday.

C Read this dialogue, then answer the questions by circling the most appropriate choice. **INTERPRETIVE**

小白： 今天是几月几号？

小李： 今天是二月二十八号。

小白： 是吗？明天是我的生日。我的生日是二月二十九号。明天晚上我请你吃晚饭，怎么样？

小李： 太好了，谢谢。可是明天不是二月二十九号。

小白： 那明天是几月几号？

小李： 明天是三月一号。你今年没有生日。

1 Which of these statements is true?

   a Little Bai has been expecting her birthday all week.

   b Little Bai almost forgot that her birthday was coming up.

   c Little Li has been expecting Little Bai's birthday.

2 What will tomorrow's date be?

   a February 28

   b February 29

   c March 1

3 Which of these statements is true?

   a Little Bai has forgotten her birthday.

   b Little Li gave the wrong date for tomorrow.

   c Little Bai's birthday is off this year's calendar.

D Complete this application form to study abroad in China. The form asks for your name in Chinese. Invent one if you don't already have one. INTERPRETIVE

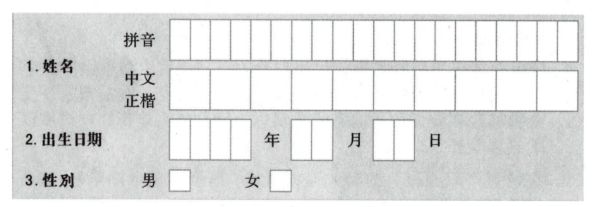

Writing and Grammar

A Write the common radical and the characters, then provide the characters' meanings. Consider their relationship with the radical.

期　明

1

2 _____

3 _____

B Rewrite these date and time phrases in Chinese characters. PRESENTATIONAL

1 November 12 _____

2 Friday evening _____

3 7:00 this evening _____

4 8:30 p.m. Saturday _____

5 a quarter after nine _____

C Complete these exchanges. PRESENTATIONAL

1 Q: 今天（是）几月几号？

A: _____ 。

2 Q: 你的生日（是）_____ ？

A: 我的生日（是）_____ 。

3 Q: 你今年多大？

A: _____ 。

4 Q: 现在几点？

A: 现在 _____ 。

5 Q: _____ ？

A: 我五点三刻吃晚饭。

D Write out the questions using "A-not-A" form, following the example below. PRESENTATIONAL

Q: 王先生是不是北京人？

A: 王先生是北京人。

1 Q: _____

A: 小李没有弟弟。

2 Q: _____

A: 小王不喜欢吃美国菜。

3 Q: _____

A: 小高的姐姐工作。

4 Q: _____

A: 高律师明天很忙。

E Based on Textbook Dialogue 2, answer these questions with 因为. INTERPERSONAL

1 白英爱为什么请高文中吃饭?

_____

2 白英爱为什么问 (to ask) 王朋忙不忙?

_____

3 王朋为什么认识李友?

_____

F Rewrite these sentences using 还, following the example below. PRESENTATIONAL

我有一个哥哥。我有一个弟弟。

我有一个哥哥,还有一个弟弟。

1 她喜欢吃中国菜。她喜欢吃美国菜。

_____

2 他认识王朋。他认识李友。

_____

3 白英爱有她哥哥的照片。白英爱有她妹妹的照片。

_____

G Translate these sentences into Chinese. PRESENTATIONAL

1 **Student A:** What time is it right now?

_____

   Student B: It's 8:45.

_____

2 **Student A:** Are you busy or not this evening?

_____

   Student B: I have things to do this evening, but am available tomorrow evening.

_____

3 **Student A:** Does your brother have a girlfriend or not?

_____

   Student B: He doesn't.

_____

   Student A: Great! I'd like to invite him to dinner on Friday.

_____

   Student B: He's busy on Friday, but I am free.

_____

   Student A: Really? But I like your brother, not you.

_____

H Write a birthday party invitation card in Chinese. Make sure to mention the date, the day of the week, the time, the food you will serve, and that you will be hosting at home. PRESENTATIONAL

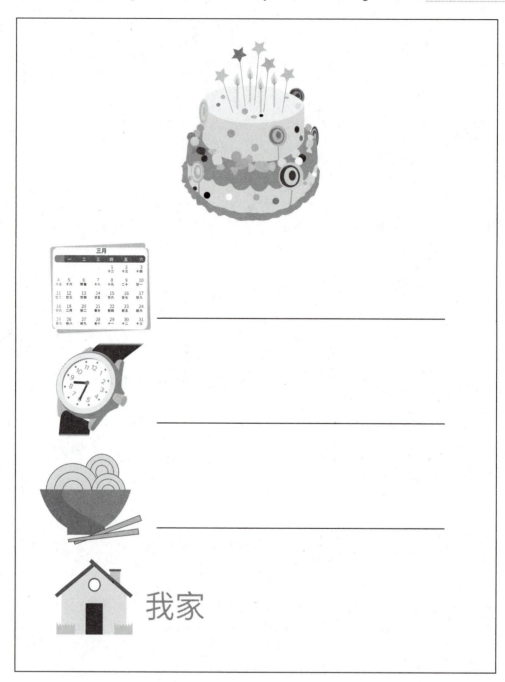

I Write a note to your friend inviting him/her to have dinner with you tomorrow to celebrate your birthday. PRESENTATIONAL

爱好
Hobbies

 Check off the following items as you learn them.

Useful Expressions

[ ] Long time no see.

[ ] How are you?

[ ] What do you like to do on weekends?

[ ] I like watching movies.

[ ] Really? Great!

Cultural Norms

[ ] Diminutives

[ ] Restaurant etiquette

[ ] Popular pastimes

As you progress through the lesson, note other useful expressions and cultural norms you would like to learn.

_____

_____

_____

Dialogue 1: Discussing Hobbies

Audio

A Listen to the Textbook Dialogue 1 audio, then mark these statements true or false. **INTERPRETIVE**

1 ____ Gao Wenzhong likes music.

2 ____ Bai Ying'ai reads a lot every weekend.

3 ____ Bai Ying'ai likes to sing and dance on weekends.

4 ____ Both Gao Wenzhong and Bai Ying'ai seem to like going to the movies.

5 ____ Gao Wenzhong is inviting Bai Ying'ai to dinner and a movie tonight.

6 ____ Gao Wenzhong and Bai Ying'ai will be joined by two friends.

B Listen to the Workbook Dialogue 1 audio, then circle the most appropriate choice. **INTERPRETIVE**

1 What does the man like to do most?

   a   listen to music

   b   play ball

   c   go to the movies

   d   go dancing

2 If the man and the woman decide to do something together, where are they most likely to go?

   a   a movie

   b   a concert

   c   a dance

   d   a ball game

C Listen to the Workbook Dialogue 2 audio, then circle the most appropriate choice. **INTERPRETIVE**

1 What does the man invite the woman to?

   a   dinner

   b   a movie

   c   a dance

   d   a concert

2 Why does the man ask the woman out?

   a   She invited him to dinner previously.

   b   She likes watching movies.

   c   Tomorrow is his birthday.

   d   He has a lot of free time.

3 Which of these statements is true?

    a   The woman doesn't accept the invitation although she isn't busy tomorrow.

    b   The woman doesn't accept the invitation because she'll be busy tomorrow.

    c   The woman accepts the invitation although she'll be busy tomorrow.

    d   The woman accepts the invitation because she isn't busy tomorrow.

Pinyin and Tone

A Identify the characters with the same initials (either *d* or *t*) and write them in *pinyin*.

对　电　跳　听　打　天

1 *d:* _____

2 *t:* _____

B Compare the tones of these characters. Indicate the tones with 1 (first tone), 2 (second tone), 3 (third tone), 4 (fourth tone), or 0 (neutral tone).

1 打 _____ 大 _____   4 歌 _____ 哥 _____

2 电 _____ 点 _____   5 舞 _____ 五 _____

3 视 _____ 是 _____   6 唱 _____ 常 _____

Speaking

A Answer these questions in Chinese based on Textbook Dialogue 1. PRESENTATIONAL

1 What does Gao Wenzhong like to do on weekends?

2 What does Bai Ying'ai like to do on weekends?

3 What will Bai Ying'ai and Gao Wenzhong do this evening?

4 Who is treating this evening?

5 Who else might also go this evening?

B Discuss your interests and hobbies with your friends, then invite them to an event on social media based on your common interests. INTERPERSONAL

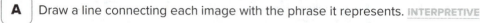

A Draw a line connecting each image with the phrase it represents. INTERPRETIVE

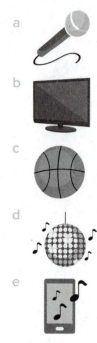

a

b

c

d

e

1 打球

2 跳舞

3 唱歌

4 听音乐

5 看电视

B Read this paragraph, then indicate Little Gao's activities on the day planner in English. Note the activities, what time they will occur, and the people who are coming. INTERPRETIVE

这个星期小高晚上都很忙。今天星期一，晚上八点小高请朋友跳舞，明天晚上六点半请同学吃饭，星期三晚上九点一刻请女朋友看电影，星期四晚上打球，星期五晚上唱歌。那周末他做什么呢？看书吗？不对！小高不喜欢看书，周末那两天他看电视，看电视，看电视……

Monday	Tuesday	Wednesday	Thursday	Friday	Saturday	Sunday

C Read this passage, then answer the questions in English. INTERPRETIVE

我大哥认识一个女孩子，她的名字叫李明英。李小姐今年二十岁，是大学生。我大哥很喜欢她，常常请她吃晚饭。周末两个人喜欢去跳舞、看电影。可是李小姐的爸爸和妈妈不喜欢我大哥，因为他今年三十八岁，可是没有工作。我也不喜欢他们两个人做男女朋友，因为李小姐是我的同学。

1 What three things do we know about Miss Li?

_____

2 What do Miss Li and the narrator's older brother like to do on weekends?

_____

3 What are the two reasons that Miss Li's parents don't like their daughter dating the narrator's older brother?

_____

4 What's the narrator's attitude toward the relationship? Why does she feel this way?

_____

D What listings are referred to in this newspaper clipping? What dates were the listings good for? INTERPRETIVE

电视电影节目表
7月13日(星期二)——7月14日(星期三)

Writing and Grammar

A Write the characters from the group below that are formed with the top-bottom pattern, then provide each character's meaning (consult a dictionary if needed).

周　音　做　作　客　那　常　是

1 ☐ _____   3 ☐ _____

2 ☐ _____   4 ☐ _____

B In the blanks, report on what these four characters like and don't like to do. PRESENTATIONAL

1 _____

2 _____

3 _____

4 _____

C Use a word or phrase from each of these four groups to make four sentences based on Chinese word order: subject + time + verb + object. PRESENTATIONAL

美国菜，球，音乐，电影

明天晚上，这个周末，星期四，今天

去看，去听，去打，去吃

我们，我爸爸妈妈，小白和小高，王朋和李友

1 _____

2 _____

3 _____

4 _____

D Translate these sentences into Chinese. PRESENTATIONAL

1 Q: Do you often see movies on weekends?

_____

A: I am busy on weekends. I work.

_____

2 Q: I'll take you dancing tonight. How about it?

_____

A: Thanks. But I don't like dancing.

_____

3 Q: What do you like to do?

_____

A: Sometimes I like to read. Sometimes I also like listening to music.

_____

4 Q: Why is it your treat today?

_____

A: Because it was your treat yesterday. It's my treat today.

_____

5 Q: You like watching foreign films, right?

_____

A: That's correct. I often watch foreign films.

_____

E | Fill in the blanks according to your circumstances. PRESENTATIONAL

我姓_____，叫_____，是_____学生。我家有_____口人，_____和我。我爸爸是_____，妈妈是_____。

我喜欢_____，有的时候也喜欢_____，可是我不喜欢_____。我周末_____忙，常常_____。

Dialogue 2: Let's Play Ball

Listening Comprehension

A Listen to the Textbook Dialogue 2 audio, then mark these statements true or false. INTERPRETIVE

1 _____ Gao Wenzhong does not like playing ball.

2 _____ Wang Peng wants to play ball this weekend.

3 _____ Gao Wenzhong is very interested in watching a ball game.

4 _____ Wang Peng is going out to eat with Gao Wenzhong.

5 _____ Gao Wenzhong likes to sleep.

6 _____ In the end, Wang Peng gives up on the idea of going out with Gao Wenzhong.

B Listen to the Workbook Dialogue 1 audio, then mark these statements true or false. INTERPRETIVE

1 _____ The woman doesn't like Chinese movies because her Chinese isn't good enough.

2 _____ The woman prefers American movies over Chinese movies.

3 _____ The man agrees that American movies are more interesting.

C Listen to the Workbook Dialogue 2 audio, then mark these statements true or false. INTERPRETIVE

1 _____ The woman invites the man to a concert.

2 _____ The man wants to play ball.

3 _____ The man invites the woman to go dancing.

D Listen to the Workbook Narrative audio, then circle the most appropriate choice. INTERPRETIVE

1 Where does the speaker spend most of his spare time?
   a at movie theaters
   b at concert halls
   c in front of the TV
   d at the library

2 What does Wang Peng like?
   a movies and TV
   b dancing and reading
   c dancing and music
   d only books

3 Which of these statements about the speaker and Wang Peng is true?

   a Wang Peng likes to read.

   b The speaker likes to watch TV.

   c Both the speaker and Wang Peng like to dance.

   d Wang Peng and the speaker are classmates.

Pinyin and Tone

A Identify the characters with the same finals (either *ie* or *iu*) and write them in *pinyin*.

别 谢 久 姐 纽 球

1 *ie:* _____

2 *iu:* _____

B Compare the tones of these characters. Indicate the tones with 1 (first tone), 2 (second tone), 3 (third tone), 4 (fourth tone), or 0 (neutral tone).

1 九 _____ 久 _____

2 思 _____ 四 _____

3 睡 _____ 水 _____

Speaking

A Answer these questions in Chinese based on Textbook Dialogue 2. PRESENTATIONAL

  1 How does Wang Peng greet Gao Wenzhong?

  2 Does Gao Wenzhong want to play ball? Why?

  3 Does Gao Wenzhong want to go to the movies? Why?

  4 What does Gao Wenzhong like to do?

  5 What did Wang Peng finally decide to do this weekend?

B In pairs, role-play a conversation. Your partner is inviting you to do something. Keep rejecting your partner's suggestions and give reasons why you do not like those activities. INTERPERSONAL

A Match the questions on the left with the appropriate replies on the right. INTERPRETIVE

1 _____ 你叫什么名字？　　a 我明天不忙。

2 _____ 这是你弟弟吗？　　b 今天晚上我很忙。

3 _____ 你明天忙不忙？　　c 我想看一个外国
电影。

4 _____ 你认识小高吗？　　d 不，这是我哥哥。

5 _____ 你喜欢听音乐
吗？　　e 因为我喜欢吃
美国菜。

6 _____ 你为什么请我
看电影？　　f 认识，他是我
同学。

7 _____ 我们为什么不
吃中国菜？　　g 我叫王朋。

8 _____ 我们去打球，
好吗？　　h 我觉得听音乐
没有意思。

9 _____ 这个周末你做
什么？　　i 我不想打球。

10 _____ 今天晚上我去
找你，好吗？　　j 因为今天是你
的生日。

小王和小李是同学。小王是英国人，他喜欢打球、看电视和看书。小李是美国人，她喜欢听音乐、唱歌和跳舞。他们都喜欢看电影，可是小王只喜欢看美国电影，小李觉得美国电影没有意思，只喜欢看外国电影。她觉得中国电影很有意思。

1 What activities does Little Wang enjoy?
   a watching TV and listening to music
   b watching Chinese movies and dancing
   c watching American movies and singing
   d playing ball and reading

2 What does Little Li like to do?
   a watching TV and listening to music
   b watching Chinese movies and dancing
   c watching American movies and dancing
   d playing ball and reading

3 Which of the following statements is true?
   a Little Wang and Little Li both like to watch TV.
   b Little Wang is American and he likes American movies.
   c Little Li is Chinese but she likes American movies.
   d Little Wang and Little Li go to the same school.

4 If Little Wang and Little Li want to do something they are both interested in, where can they go?
   a to a ball game
   b to a library
   c to a dance party
   d none of the above

C Read this dialogue, then mark the statements true or false. INTERPRETIVE

小王：你喜欢看美国电影还是外国电影?

老李：我不喜欢看美国电影，也不喜欢看外国电影。

小王： 你觉得中国音乐有意思还是美国音乐有意思？

老李： 我觉得中国音乐和美国音乐都没有意思。

小王： 你常常看中文书还是英文书？

老李： 我不看中文书，也不看英文书。

小王： 那你喜欢吃中国菜还是美国菜？

老李： 中国菜和美国菜我都喜欢吃。

1 ___ This conversation most likely takes place in the United States.

2 ___ Old Li likes European movies, not American movies.

3 ___ Old Li feels that both Chinese music and American music are boring.

4 ___ When Old Li reads, the book must be in a language other than English or Chinese.

5 ___ It seems Old Li does not like anything American or Chinese.

D Read this passage, then answer the questions in English. INTERPRETIVE

小李很喜欢打球，可是他的女朋友小文觉得打球没有意思，她只喜欢看电影。明天是星期六，也是小文的生日。小李和小文想去看电影。可是看什么电影呢？小李觉得 «The Benchwarmers» 这个电影有很多人打球，很有意思。小文不喜欢打球，可是也想去看那个电影。小李和小文都很高兴，他们明天下午三点半去看电影。

1 What does Little Li like to do?

_____

2 Why does Little Li want to see a movie with Little Wen tomorrow?

_____

3 What makes the movie *The Benchwarmers* special to Little Li?

_____

4 Why are both Little Li and Little Wen happy?

_____

E Locate the channels for movies and music, respectively, on this Chinese TV guide. INTERPRETIVE

今明电视节目安排

8月1日 周一电视

第一电视台-1(综合频道)

19:55 电视剧:冼星海(5、6)
21:40 纪实十分

第二电视台-2(经济频道)

20:25 经济与法
21:30 经济半小时

第三电视台-3(综艺频道)

18:30 综艺快报
19:05 动物世界
21:15 快乐驿站

第四电视台-4(国际频道)

20:10 走遍中国
20:40 海峡两岸
21:00 中国新闻
21:30 今日关注
22:00 中国文艺

第五电视台-5(体育频道)

18:55 巅峰时刻
21:30 体育世界

第六电视台-6(电影频道)

21:48 世界电影之旅之资讯快车

第八电视台-8(电视剧频道)

19:30 电视剧:国家机密(15—17)

第十电视台-10(科教频道)

20:10 历程
20:30 走近科学
21:40 讲述

第十二电视台-12(社会与法频道)

20:00 大家看法
23:10 心理访谈
23:30 电视剧:公安局长(7、8)

第十三电视台-新闻频道

20:30 新闻会客厅
21:30 国际观察
21:55 天气资讯

第十四电视台-少儿频道

19:00 中国动画(精品版)
19:30 智慧树
20:00 动漫世界

第十五电视台-音乐频道

20:10 经典

A Identify the patterns of 我 and 找, then write the characters that share the same pattern from the group below.

错 久 睡 不 别 人

1 我

2 找

B Rearrange these Chinese words into sentences, using the English sentences as clues. PRESENTATIONAL

1 觉得 | 这个 | 没有 | 电影 | 有 | 意思 | 你
(Do you think this movie is interesting?)

2 王朋 | 去 | 周末 | 和 | 李友 | 这个 | 打球
(Wang Peng and Li You will go play ball this weekend.)

3 今天晚上 | 他 | 看 | 电视 | 想 | 不 | 听 | 音乐 | 想
(Tonight he wants to watch TV, not listen to music.)

Based on Textbook Dialogue 2, answer these questions using 因为…所以…. INTERPERSONAL

1 Q: 高文中为什么请白英爱看电影？

A: _____

2 Q: 高文中为什么不想去打球？

A: _____

3 Q: 高文中为什么不想去看球？

A: _____

D Answer these questions according to your own circumstances. INTERPERSONAL

1 Q: 你周末常常做什么？

A: _____

2 Q: 你喜欢看美国电影还是外国电影？

A: _____

3 Q: 你今天晚上想几点睡觉？

A: _____

4 Q: 你觉得打球有意思还是跳舞有意思？

A: _____

E Translate these sentences into Chinese. PRESENTATIONAL

1 Student A: Little Wang, long time no see. Are you busy?

_____

Student B: Long time no see, Little Gao. I've been busy. How about you?

_____

Student A: I'm busy, too.

_____

2 Student A: Let's go dancing this weekend, OK?

_____

Student B: I don't want to go. I only want to get some sleep.

_____

3 Student A: I'd like to take you to see a foreign film.

_____

Student B: Thank you. But I think foreign films are boring.

_____

Student A: Never mind. I'll go find someone else.

_____

4 Student A: What would you like to do tonight? How about watching TV?

_____

Student B: I think watching TV is boring. I like singing and dancing. I'd like to go singing tonight.

_____

Student A: OK.

_____

5 Student A: Today is my birthday. I am nineteen years old. My friends will take me out for dinner and dancing tonight.

_____

Student B: You like dancing, right?

_____

Student A: Right, I like dancing. I often dance on weekends. How about you?

_____

Student B: I think dancing is boring.

_____

Student A: Is that so?!

_____

F   Based on the chart, report on Little Wang's plans for next week. PRESENTATIONAL

Monday	Tuesday	Wednesday	Thursday	Friday	Saturday	Sunday

_____

_____

_____

_____

看朋友
Visiting Friends

 Check off the following items as you learn them.

Useful Expressions

[ ] Who is it?

[ ] Please come in!

[ ] Let me introduce you to each other.

[ ] Pleased to meet you!

[ ] I'm sorry.

Cultural Norms

[ ] Visiting etiquette

[ ] Standard greetings

[ ] Classification of tea

[ ] Popular beverages

As you progress through the lesson, note other useful expressions and cultural norms you would like to learn.

_____

_____

_____

Dialogue: Visiting a Friend's Place

Audio

Listening Comprehension

A Listen to the Textbook Dialogue audio, then mark these statements true or false. INTERPRETIVE

1 _____ Wang Peng and Li You had met Gao Wenzhong's older sister before.

2 _____ Li You was very happy to meet Gao Wenzhong's sister.

3 _____ Gao Wenzhong's sister is a student.

4 _____ Li You likes to drink tea.

5 _____ Gao Wenzhong's sister gave Li You a cola.

B Listen to the Workbook Dialogue 1 audio, then mark these statements true or false. INTERPRETIVE

1 _____ The man and the woman are speaking on the phone.

2 _____ The man and the woman have never met each other before.

3 _____ The man is looking for his younger brother.

C Listen to the Workbook Dialogue 2 audio, then circle the most appropriate choice. INTERPRETIVE

1 The dialogue most likely takes place between

a two strangers.

b a parent and a child.

c two friends.

d a teacher and a student.

2 Which of these statements about the woman is true?

a She doesn't like TV in general but she likes what is on TV tonight.

b She doesn't like TV in general and she likes what is on TV tonight even less.

c She likes TV in general but she doesn't like what is on TV tonight.

d She likes TV in general and she particularly likes what is on TV tonight.

3 What will they most likely end up doing?

a watching TV

b seeing a Chinese movie

c reading an American novel

d listening to Chinese music

Listen to the Workbook Dialogue 3 audio, then circle the most appropriate choice. INTERPRETIVE

1 Which of the following is the correct order of the woman's preferences?

a coffee, tea

b cola, coffee

c coffee, cola

d tea, coffee

2 Which beverage does the man not have?

a tea

b water

c cola

d coffee

3 Which beverage does the woman finally get?

a tea

b water

c cola

d coffee

Pinyin and Tone

A Identify the characters with the same initials (either *j* or *z*) and write them in *pinyin*.

进　在　子　介　坐　见

1 *j*: _____

2 *z*: _____

B Compare the tones of these characters. Indicate the tones with 1 (first tone), 2 (second tone), 3 (third tone), 4 (fourth tone), or 0 (neutral tone).

1 介 _____ 姐 _____   **4** 哪 _____ 那 _____

2 进 _____ 今 _____   **5** 喝 _____ 和 _____

3 吧 _____ 爸 _____   **6** 做 _____ 坐 _____

A Answer these questions in Chinese based on the Textbook Dialogue. PRESENTATIONAL

1 Who went to Gao Wenzhong's house?

2 Had Wang Peng and Li You met Gao Wenzhong's sister before?

3 What is Gao Wenzhong's older sister's name?

4 How is Gao Wenzhong's house?

5 Where does Gao Wenzhong's older sister work?

6 What did Wang Peng want to drink?

7 Why did Li You ask for a glass of water?

B In pairs, role-play meeting someone for the first time. Exchange basic greetings, ask the other person his/her name, profession (or if he/she is a student), and hobbies. INTERPERSONAL

C In pairs, role-play visiting a friend's home. Compliment your friend's house. Your friend offers you coffee or tea, but you just want a glass of water. INTERPERSONAL

Reading Comprehension

A Read this description, then match the people with their preferred beverages. INTERPRETIVE

小高、小白和小王都是同学。小高不喜欢喝咖啡，也不喜欢喝茶。小白不喝可乐，也不常喝咖啡。小王只喜欢喝咖啡。

1	____ Little Gao	a	tea
2	____ Little Bai	b	coffee
3	____ Little Wang	c	cola

Read this dialogue, then mark the statements true or false. **INTERPRETIVE**

（王中去他的同学李文家玩儿。）

李文：王中，你想喝点儿什么？

王中：给我一瓶可乐吧。

李文：对不起，我家没有可乐。

王中：那给我一杯茶，好吗？

李文：对不起，也没有茶。

王中：那我喝一杯咖啡吧。

李文：对不起，我只有水。

王中：你家很大，也很漂亮，可是……

1 ____ Wang Zhong is visiting Li Wen's home.

2 ____ Wang Zhong seems to like tea better than water.

3 ____ Li Wen's refrigerator is full of all kinds of beverages.

4 ____ Wang Zhong is impressed by the beverages that Li Wen has offered.

C You have ninety Taiwan dollars. What three beverages can you order from this menu? INTERPRETIVE

1 _____

2 _____

3 _____

饮料

可乐/雪碧/健怡可乐 .... M $25 L $30

柳橙汁 .... M $35

鲜榨柳橙汁 .... M $50

摩斯矿泉水 .... M $18

冰咖啡/冰红茶 .... M $30 L $35

热咖啡/热红茶 .... M $30

奇异蔬果汁 .... M $50

可可亚 (季节限定) .... M $30

咖啡欧蕾 (季节限定) .... M $30

Writing and Grammar

A Each of these characters shares the same radical, 口. Write the *pinyin* for the characters in the top row, compare them with the *pinyin* of the characters below, then consider the relationship between each pair.

1 呀 _____   2 哪 _____   3 啡 _____   4 吧 _____

牙 (yá)   那 (nà)   非 (fēi)   巴 (bā)

B Describe the images by writing the appropriate numbers, measure words, and nouns. PRESENTATIONAL

1   2   3

_____   _____   _____

Rearrange these Chinese words into sentences, using the English sentences as clues. PRESENTATIONAL

1 常常 ｜ 王老师 ｜ 在学校 ｜ 看书
(Professor Wang often reads at school.)

_____

2 看电视 ｜ 周末 ｜ 我的同学 ｜ 在家
(My classmate watches TV at home on weekends.)

_____

3 小白 ｜ 工作 ｜ 星期五 ｜ 在哪儿
(Where does Little Bai work on Fridays?)

_____

D Answer these questions affirmatively and negatively, then circle the response that is true for you personally. PRESENTATIONAL

1 你的老师高不高?

Affirmative: _____

Negative: _____

2 你的医生好不好?

Affirmative: _____

Negative: _____

3 你的英文书有没有意思?

Affirmative: _____

Negative: _____

4 你今天高兴不高兴?

Affirmative: _____

Negative: _____

5 你家大吗？

Affirmative: _____

Negative: _____

6 你们的学校漂亮吗？

Affirmative: _____

Negative: _____

E The following is part of a conversation between Little Li, a waiter, and Mr. Gao, a customer. Complete the conversation by inserting the correct phrases or sentences listed below.
PRESENTATIONAL

1 您要英国茶还是中国茶

2 可以，可以

3 好久不见

4 请坐，请坐

5 高先生

6 请进，请进

7 您想喝点什么

Little Li: _____，_____。

Mr Gao: 小李，好久不见。

Little Li: _____。

Mr Gao: 好，谢谢。

Little Li: _____。

Mr. Gao: 我不想坐这儿，我想坐那儿。可以吗？

Little Li: _____。

Little Li: _____?

Mr. Gao: 我想喝茶。

Little Li: _____?

Mr. Gao: 给我一杯英国茶吧!

F Translate these exchanges into Chinese. PRESENTATIONAL

1 Student A: Let me introduce you to each other. This is my classmate, Li Ming.

_____

_____

Student B: Mr. Li, my name is Wang Ying. Pleased to meet you.

_____

_____

Student C: Miss Wang, very pleased to meet you, too.

_____

2 Student A: Where do you work?

_____

Student B: I work at a school.

_____

3 Student A: What would you like to do this weekend? See a movie or go dancing?

_____

Student B: Let's go dancing!

_____

4 **Student A:** Would you like to have something to drink? Coffee or tea?

_____

Student B: I'll have a cup of coffee.

_____

G You write an etiquette blog for tourists traveling to China. List five need-to-know expressions for hosts and guests. PRESENTATIONAL

Welcoming Host   **Gracious Guest**

_____   _____

_____   _____

_____   _____

_____   _____

Narrative: At a Friend's Place

Audio

Listening Comprehension

A Listen to the Textbook Narrative audio, then mark these statements true or false. INTERPRETIVE

1 _____ Gao Wenzhong's older sister works in a library.

2 _____ Wang Peng had two glasses of water at Wenzhong's house.

3 _____ Li You did not drink tea at Wenzhong's house.

4 _____ Wang Peng and Li You chatted and watched TV at Wenzhong's house.

5 _____ Wang Peng and Li You left Wenzhong's house at noon.

B Listen to the Workbook Narrative audio, then mark these statements true or false. INTERPRETIVE

1 _____ The speaker thinks that Little Bai and Little Li are old friends.

2 _____ The three people are most likely at the speaker's place.

3 _____ Little Bai told Little Li that he works in the library.

C Listen to the Workbook Dialogue audio, then circle the most appropriate choice. INTERPRETIVE

1 Where were little Bai and his younger brother Saturday night?

 a at home

 b at Little Gao's place

 c at Little Li's place

 d at Little Bai's brother's place

2 What did Little Bai's brother do at the party?

 a He had tea.

 b He watched TV.

 c He chatted with friends.

 d He danced.

3 How did Little Bai spend most of the evening?

 a drinking tea and watching TV

 b chatting and watching TV

 c drinking tea and chatting

 d drinking tea, chatting, and watching TV

A Identify the characters with the same finals (either *uan* or *iao*) and write them in *pinyin*.

欢　算　聊　馆　跳　叫

1 *iao:* _____

2 *uan:* _____

B Compare the tones of these characters. Indicate the tones with 1 (first tone), 2 (second tone), 3 (third tone), 4 (fourth tone), or 0 (neutral tone).

1 玩 _____ 晚 _____　　**2** 了 _____ 乐 _____

Speaking

A Answer these questions in Chinese based on the Textbook Narrative. PRESENTATIONAL

1 Why did Wang Peng and Li You go to Gao Wenzhong's house?

2 Where does Gao Wenzhong's sister work?

3 What did Wang Peng drink? How much?

4 What did Wang Peng and Li You do at Gao Wenzhong's house?

5 When did Wang Peng and Li You go home?

B In pairs, ask each other what beverage you had last night, how much, and what else you did. Then present the information you've gathered. INTERPERSONAL & PRESENTATIONAL

A Read this note, then answer the questions in English. INTERPRETIVE

小张：

　　明天晚上七点半学校有一个中国电影，
我们一起去看，好吗？我明天晚上来找你。

　　　　　　　小高
　　　　　　　十月五日晚上九点半

1 Who wrote the note?

_____

2 What time is the movie?

_____

3 Where is the movie?

_____

4 When will the two friends meet?

_____

5 When was the note written?

_____

昨天是小李的生日，小李请了小高、小张和王朋三个同学去她家吃饭。他们七点吃晚饭。小李的家不大，可是很漂亮。小李的爸爸是老师，他很有意思。小李的妈妈是医生，昨天很忙，九点才回家吃晚饭。小李的哥哥和姐姐都不在家吃饭。王朋和小李的爸爸妈妈一起喝茶、聊天。小高、小张和小李一起喝可乐、看电视。小高、小张和王朋十一点才回家。

1 _____ Little Li's home is both large and beautiful.

2 _____ Little Li celebrated her birthday with her classmates but not with her entire family.

3 _____ Wang Peng drank cola with his friends.

4 _____ Little Li's friends left her home about the same time.

C   Based on the passage in (B), circle the most appropriate choice.

1 Who was late for dinner last night?
   a   Little Gao
   b   Little Zhang
   c   Little Li's father
   d   Little Li's mother

2 Which of the following statements is true?
   a   Little Li's mother is a teacher.
   b   Little Li's father is an interesting person.
   c   Little Li's brother and sister were home last night.
   d   Wang Peng talked with Little Li all evening.

今天小高去找他的同学小王，小王的妹妹也在家。可是小高不认识小王的妹妹。小王介绍了一下。小王的妹妹也是他们学校的学生。她很漂亮，喜欢唱歌和看书。这个周末小高想请小王的妹妹去喝咖啡、看电影。

1 ____ Little Gao has met Little Wang's sister before.

2 ____ Little Gao and Little Wang's sister attend the same school.

3 ____ Little Gao's sister likes to dance.

4 ____ Little Gao would like to invite Little Wang and his sister to see a movie this weekend.

Writing and Grammar

A Which of these characters are based on the left-right pattern, and which on the enclosing pattern? After filling in the answers, write the characters in the spaces provided.

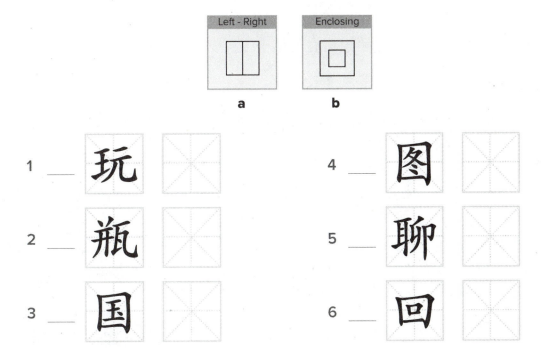

Left - Right

Enclosing

a   b

1 ___ 玩

2 ___ 瓶

3 ___ 国

4 ___ 图

5 ___ 聊

6 ___ 回

B This chart shows what Little Gao did and didn't do last night. Write questions-and-answers based on the information provided, following the example below. PRESENTATIONAL

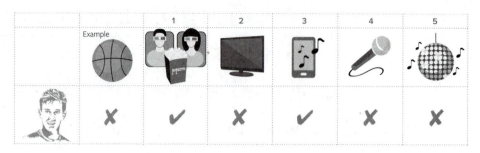

Q: 他昨天晚上打球了吗？

A: 他昨天晚上没打球。

1 Q: _____

A: _____

2 Q: _____

A: _____

3 Q: _____

A: _____

4 Q: _____

A: _____

5 Q: _____

A: _____

C Based on the images, form questions'-and-answers about the beverages Little Wang drank at the party. Follow the example below. PRESENTATIONAL

Q: 他喝咖啡了吗？

A: 他喝咖啡了。

Q: 他喝了几杯咖啡？

A: 他喝了两杯咖啡。

1 Q: _____

   A: _____

   Q: _____

   A: _____

2 Q: _____

   A: _____

   Q: _____

   A: _____

3 Q: _____

   A: _____

   Q: _____

   A: _____

D Little Li is always late. Summarize what her friends have told you about her habits, following the example below. PRESENTATIONAL

6:00 p.m.　　　吃晚饭　　　6:30 p.m.

我们六点吃晚饭，她六点半才来。

1 7:30 p.m.　　看电影　　　7:45 p.m.

_____

2 8:00 a.m.　　工作　　　8:15 a.m.

_____

3 6:30 p.m.　　打球　　　7:00 p.m.

_____

Translate these sentences into Chinese.

1 **Q:** Did you play ball last night?

_____

A: No, I didn't. I was too busy.

_____

2 **Q:** Did you have coffee?

_____

A: I didn't. I only drank two glasses of water.

_____

3 **Q:** Why didn't you go to bed until 12:00 a.m.?

_____

A: Because I saw two movies, and didn't go home until 11:30 p.m.

_____

_____

4 I first met Gao Wenzhong at the library. He is tall and from England. He likes to chat. We often chat and have tea together. He thinks dancing is fun. I will take him dancing tonight.

_____

_____

_____

_____

F Describe a recent visit to a friend's place. Mention what you did and what beverages you had.
PRESENTATIONAL

Bringing It Together (Lessons 1–5)

Pinyin and Tone

A Compare the characters' pronunciation and tones, then write them in *pinyin*.

1 你们_____   你好_____

2 不错_____   不来_____

3 音乐_____   可乐_____

4 觉得_____   睡觉_____

Radicals

A Group these characters according to their radicals.

喝	馆	孩	打	晚	星	绍	快	说	找
今	时	国	他	图	睡	吃	杯	学	妹
呢	们	忙	谁	姓	看	给	样	饭	回

Radical   **Characters**

1 _____   _____

2 _____   _____

3 _____   _____

4 _____   _____

5 _____   _____

6 _____   _____

7 _____ _____

8 _____ _____

9 _____ _____

10 _____ _____

11 _____ _____

12 _____ _____

13 _____ _____

VO Compounds

A Circle the verbs that are VO compounds.

吃饭　　跳舞　　工作　　认识　　请客

Communication

A Interview your classmates, jot down the information you gather, then present an oral or written report to introduce them to the class. Below are sample questions to help you get started.

Personal and Family Background

1 你今年多大？

_____

2 你的生日（是）几月几号？

_____

3 你是纽约人吗？ _____

4 你家有几口人？有没有兄 (xiōng) (older brother) 弟姐妹？

_____

5 你爸爸、妈妈做什么工作？他们在哪儿工作？

_____

Likes and Dislikes

1 你喜欢做什么？打球还是看电影？

_____

2 你觉得做什么有意思／没有意思？

_____

3 你喜欢听音乐吗？_____

4 你喜欢听谁的音乐？_____

5 你喜欢跳舞吗？_____

6 你喜欢跳什么舞？_____

7 你喜欢喝什么？水、茶、可乐还是咖啡？

_____

Habits and Routines

1 你常常看电视吗？_____

2 你常常在哪儿看书？_____

3 你晚上常常几点睡觉？_____

4 你周末常常做什么？_____

约 时 间
Making Appointments

 Check off the following items as you learn them.

Useful Expressions

- 〔 〕 What's going on?
- 〔 〕 Are you free tomorrow?
- 〔 〕 I'll wait for your call.
- 〔 〕 No problem.
- 〔 〕 You're welcome.

Cultural Norms

- 〔 〕 Honorifics
- 〔 〕 Phone etiquette
- 〔 〕 Popular messaging apps
- 〔 〕 China Standard Time (CST)

As you progress through the lesson, note other useful expressions and cultural norms you would like to learn.

_____

_____

_____

Dialogue 1: Calling Your Teacher

Audio

A Listen to the Textbook Dialogue 1 audio, then circle the most appropriate choice. INTERPRETIVE

1 Why is Li You calling Teacher Chang?
- a Li You cannot come to school because she is sick.
- b Li You wants to ask some questions.
- c Li You wants to know where Teacher Chang's office is.
- d Li You wants to know where the meeting is.

2 What is Teacher Chang going to do this afternoon?
- a teach two classes
- b go home early
- c attend a meeting
- d go to a doctor's appointment

3 How many classes will Teacher Chang teach tomorrow morning?
- a one
- b two
- c three
- d four

4 What will Teacher Chang be doing at 3:30 tomorrow afternoon?
- a attending a meeting
- b giving an exam
- c working in her office
- d seeing a doctor

5 Where is Li You going to meet Teacher Chang?
- a in Teacher Chang's office
- b in the classroom
- c in the meeting room
- d in the library

6 When will Li You meet with Teacher Chang tomorrow?
- a 9:00 a.m.
- b 10:30 a.m.
- c 3:00 p.m.
- d 4:30 p.m.

B Listen to the Workbook Dialogue 1 audio, then mark these statements true or false. INTERPRETIVE

1 _____ The woman in the dialogue is the caller's sister.

2 _____ The caller asks to speak to Little Gao.

3 _____ A Chinese film will be screened tonight.

4 _____ The woman will most likely stay home tonight.

C Listen to the Workbook Dialogue 2 audio, then circle the most appropriate choice. INTERPRETIVE

1 Which of the following statements is true?

a The woman invites the man to a dinner party at her home.

b The woman invites the man to a dance at her home.

c The woman hopes to go to a dinner party at the man's home.

d The woman hopes to go to a dance at the man's home.

2 Why does the man choose not to go?

a Because he is hosting a party.

b Because he has to prepare for a test.

c Because he is not allowed to go.

d Because he doesn't like the host.

Pinyin and Tone

A Identify the characters with the same initials (either *j* or *sh*) and write them in *pinyin*.

试 间 上 时 节 级

1 *j:* _____

2 *sh:* _____

B Compare the tones of these characters. Indicate the tones with 1 (first tone), 2 (second tone), 3 (third tone), 4 (fourth tone), or 0 (neutral tone).

1 以 _____ 意 _____

2 室 _____ 试 _____

3 可 _____ 课 _____

Speaking

A Answer these questions in Chinese based on Textbook Dialogue 1. PRESENTATIONAL

1 Why did Li You call Teacher Chang?

2 Will Teacher Chang be free this afternoon? Why or why not?

3 Will Teacher Chang be free tomorrow morning? Why or why not?

4 What will Teacher Chang do at three o'clock tomorrow afternoon?

5 When will Li You go to visit Teacher Chang?

B Have a conversation with your teacher. You would like to make an appointment, but he/she is busy at the time you suggest. Ask when he/she will be available. Decide on a time and place to meet. INTERPERSONAL

Reading Comprehension

A Match the sentences below with the responses that follow. INTERPRETIVE

1 _____ 你是哪位？

2 _____ 我们今天晚上去跳舞，好吗？

3 _____ 喝点儿茶，怎么样？

4 _____ 喂，请问小白在吗？

5 _____ 认识你很高兴。

6 _____ 谢谢。

7 _____ 明天见。

8 _____ 今天下午我来找你，好吗？

a 认识你们我也很高兴。

b 不客气。

c 再见。

d 对不起，我不喜欢喝茶。

e 对不起，她去图书馆了。

f 对不起，我今天下午要开会。

g 对不起，我明天要考试。

h 我是王朋。

B Read Teacher Li's schedule, then answer the questions in English. INTERPRETIVE

小高的中文老师李老师很忙。我们一起看一下她星期三做什么。

时间	活动	
8:30	到学校去上课	
9:00 - 10:00	上一年级中文课	
10:15 - 11:00	去图书馆找书	
12:00 - 1:00	在办公室吃饭	
1:30 - 2:30	上二年级中文课	
2:45 - 3:30	开会	
4:00 - 5:00	学生来她的办公室问问题	

1 李老师星期三有几节课?

_____

2 李老师的学生星期三有没有考试?

_____

3 李老师回家吃午饭 *(wǔfàn)* (lunch) 吗?

_____

4 李老师上了一年级中文课以后做什么?

_____

5 要是小高想去李老师的办公室问问题,
什么时候去方便?

_____

6 你觉得李老师星期三几点才可以回家?

_____

C Read this dialogue, then mark the statements true or false. INTERPRETIVE

（李友给王朋打电话。李友问了王朋几个
问题。）

王朋: 还有别的问题吗?

李友: 我还有一个问题。

王朋: 你问吧。

李友: 你明天下午有空吗? 我想找你聊
天儿。

王朋：对不起，我明天下午要开会。

李友：明天晚上怎么样？

王朋：我明天晚上也没有时间。我想请一个女孩子去跳舞。

李友：……那算了。

王朋：你也认识那个女孩子。

李友：是吗？她叫什么名字？

王朋：她姓李，叫李友。

1 ____ Li You's schedule for tomorrow seems quite flexible.

2 ____ Wang Peng hopes to see Li You tomorrow.

3 ____ Li You does not know the girl whom Wang Peng wants to take to the dance.

D Based on the dialogue in (C), circle the most appropriate choice.

1 What will Wang Peng do tomorrow?

  a He will have a meeting in the afternoon and chat with Li You in the evening.

  b He will meet with Li You in the afternoon and go dancing with another girl in the evening.

  c He will have a meeting in the afternoon and go dancing with Li You in the evening.

2 On hearing Wang Peng's plan for tomorrow evening, how is Li You feeling?

  a first disappointed and then very happy

  b first very happy and then disappointed

  c neither happy nor disappointed

Writing and Grammar

A Which of these characters in the group below are based on the top-bottom pattern, and which on the semi-enclosing pattern? After identifying the patterns, write the characters and their common radicals in the spaces provided (write the common radicals in 3 and 6).

 Top - Bottom

 Semi - Enclosing

a   **b**

1 ___

2 ___

3 ___

4 ___

5 ___

6 ___

B Describe the images by writing the appropriate numbers, measure words, and nouns. Follow the example below. PRESENTATIONAL

 两个问题

1   2  3  4

星期一
8:30 上课
10:00 上课
1:45 上课

_____   _____   _____   _____

C Use 要是 and the information below to form questions about how you would like to spend your free time. Follow the example below. PRESENTATIONAL

没课

Q: 要是你明天没课，你做什么？

A: 我（去）（图书馆）看书。

1 没事儿

Q: _____?

A: _____。

2 有空儿

Q: _____?

A: _____。

3 不开会

Q: _____?

A: _____。

4 不考试

Q: _____?

A: _____。

5 不工作

Q: _____?

A: _____。

D   Translate these sentences into Chinese. PRESENTATIONAL

1   Student A: I'd like to give him a call.

_____

Student B: Don't call. He is not home right now.

_____

Student A: Really? When will he be home?

_____

Student B: He won't go home until after 5:00 p.m.

_____

2 Student A: Miss Bai, do you have time tomorrow?

_____

Student B: I am free tomorrow. What's the matter?

_____

Student A: I'd like to treat you to a movie.

_____

Student B: Watching movies is boring. Let's go dancing.

_____

Student A: No problem. See you tomorrow.

_____

3 Gao Wenzhong: Hello! Is Teacher Chang there?

_____

Teacher Chang: This is she. Who's this, please?

_____

Gao Wenzhong: Teacher Chang, how are you? This is Gao Wenzhong.

_____

Teacher Chang: Hi, Gao Wenzhong, what is it?

_____

Gao Wenzhong: I'd like to go to your office right now to ask you a question. Is that okay?

_____

Teacher Chang: Sure. I'll wait for you in my office.

_____

Gao Wenzhong: Thanks.

_____

E Ask your teacher what his/her typical school day is like. Take notes and transcribe what he/she said.
PRESENTATIONAL

_____

_____

_____

Dialogue 2: Calling a Friend for Help

Listening Comprehension

A Listen to the Textbook Dialogue 2 audio, then mark these statements true or false. INTERPRETIVE

1 _____ Li You is returning Wang Peng's phone call.

2 _____ Li You has an exam next week.

3 _____ Li You asks Wang Peng to practice Chinese with her.

4 _____ Wang Peng invites Li You to have coffee.

5 _____ Wang Peng is going to have dinner with Li You this evening.

6 _____ Wang Peng does not know exactly when he is going to call Li You.

B Listen to the Workbook Dialogue 1 audio, then mark these statements true or false. INTERPRETIVE

1 _____ Tomorrow is Friday.

2 _____ Li You cannot go to the dinner tomorrow because she will be busy.

3 _____ Li You will be practicing Chinese this evening.

4 _____ Wang Peng promises to help Li You with her Chinese tomorrow at 6:30 p.m.

C Listen to the Workbook Dialogue 2 audio, then mark these statements true or false. INTERPRETIVE

1 _____ Wang Peng cannot help Li You because he has class tomorrow afternoon.

2 _____ Wang Peng asks Little Bai to help Li You with her Chinese.

3 _____ Little Bai and Li You will meet at 2 p.m. tomorrow in the library.

Pinyin and Tone

A Identify the characters with the same finals (either *ie* or *ian*) and write them in *pinyin*.

节　间　便　别　练　面

1 *ie:* _____

2 *ian:* _____

B Compare the tones of these characters. Indicate the tones with 1 (first tone), 2 (second tone), 3 (third tone), 4 (fourth tone), or 0 (neutral tone).

1 会 _____ 回 _____   3 习 _____ 喜 _____

2 问 _____ 文 _____   4 行 _____ 姓 _____

Speaking

A Answer these questions in Chinese based on Textbook Dialogue 2. PRESENTATIONAL

1 Why did Li You call Wang Peng?

2 Why did Wang Peng ask Li You to invite him for coffee?

3 What will Wang Peng do tonight?

4 Will Wang Peng meet with Li You tonight?

5 What will Li You do tonight?

B In pairs, role-play a phone call. Call your partner for a favor and promise something in return. You would like to meet him/her tonight, but he/she is going to see a movie. He/she promises to give you a call later. INTERPERSONAL

Reading Comprehension

A Review Little Gao's plans for next week, then answer the questions in English. INTERPRETIVE

1 他什么时候考中文?

_____

2 他跟王朋在哪儿练习中文?

_____

3 他为什么星期五要打电话回家?

_____

4 他星期几没事儿?

_____

5 他星期四要做什么?

_____

6 他星期天在哪儿吃饭?

_____

B Read this email, then mark the statements true or false. INTERPRETIVE

小白:

　　我下午在图书馆等你,可是你没来。我四点给你打了一个电话,可是你不在家。我们什么时候可以见面?我明天晚上要跟小王一起去看电影。要是你明天晚上有空,我可以不去看电影。今天晚上在家等你的电话。

小高

1 _____ Little Bai and Little Gao were in the library this afternoon.

2 _____ Little Bai did not leave her dorm until 4:00 p.m.

3 _____ Little Gao wants to see Little Bai.

4 _____ We do not know for sure what Little Gao will be doing tomorrow evening.

5 _____ Little Gao considers an appointment with Little Bai more important than seeing a movie with Little Wang.

6 _____ Little Gao will call Little Bai again this evening.

C Read this note that Little Bai left for Wang Peng, then answer the questions in English. INTERPRETIVE

王朋：

你今天下午没有课，我来找你，可是你不在。我昨天到常老师的办公室去，请她帮我练习说中文，可是她很忙。我今天上午给老师打电话，问她今天下午方便不方便，她说她明天下午两点以后才有空儿。我明天上午要考中文，你可以帮我准备一下吗？请你回来以后给我打电话。谢谢！

小白

五点半

1 Where did Wang Peng find this note?

_____

2 When was this note written?

_____

3 Why didn't Little Bai call before dropping by?

_____

4 Why did Little Bai go looking for Wang Peng?

_____

5 Did Little Bai get help from her teacher? Explain the situation.

_____

6 What do you think Wang Peng will do after he reads this note?

_____

D After reading the note in (C), Wang Peng found another one. Read it, then mark the statements true or false. INTERPRETIVE

王朋：

　　李友今天下午两点半给你打电话说她今天下午两点才知道星期五上午有中文考试，所以今天晚上不跟你去跳舞。要是你有空，她想请你今天下午帮她练习中文，她考试以后请你看电影。你回来以后给她打电话吧。

小高

两点三刻

1 _____ This note was left by Li You.

2 _____ Wang Peng was not in at 2:30 p.m. but was back by 2:45 p.m.

3 _____ At 1:30 p.m. today Li You still planned to go to the dance.

4 _____ We do not know when Wang Peng will call Li You back.

5 _____ Li You was certain that Wang Peng would be available this afternoon.

E Based on the note in (D), circle the most appropriate choice. INTERPRETIVE

1 Which of the statements is true?

　a Li You was told last Friday that there would be an exam.

　b Li You was told this afternoon that there would be an exam on Friday.

　c Li You was told that yesterday evening's exam was postponed till Friday.

2 When does Li You hope to take Wang Peng to a movie?

　a Wednesday evening

　b Thursday evening

　c Friday evening

Writing and Grammar

A Write the common radical and the characters, then provide the characters' meanings. Consider their relationship with the radical.

话　请　说

1 ☐

2 ☐ _____

3 ☐ _____

4 ☐ _____

B Make sentences using 别, 得, and the given words. Follow the example below. PRESENTATIONAL

Student A: 我想去找同学聊天儿。（准备考试）

Student B: <u>别</u>去找同学聊天，你<u>得</u>准备考试。

1 Student A: 我想看电视。（看书）

Student B: _____

2 Student A: 我想喝咖啡。（睡觉）

Student B: _____

3 Student A: 我想跟朋友玩儿。（工作）

Student B: _____

C Answer these questions according to your own circumstances. INTERPERSONAL

1 你常常给谁打电话？

_____

2 你是大学几年级的学生？

_____

3 你星期一有几节课？

_____

4 你星期四几点有中文课？

_____

5 你常常跟谁一起练习说中文？

_____

D Rearrange these Chinese words into sentences, using the English sentences as clues.
PRESENTATIONAL

1 四点 | 我 | 办公室 | 电话 | 在 | 明天 | 等 | 以后 | 下午 | 你的

(I will be waiting for your phone call in the office after 4:00 p.m. tomorrow.)

_____

2 朋友 | 才 | 吃饭 | 昨天晚上 | 我 | 回来 | 晚上九点 | 请我

(My friend took me out for dinner last night. I didn't come back until 9:00 p.m.)

_____

3 您 | 回来 | 给我 | 方便 | 以后 | 打 | 要是 | 电话

(If it is convenient for you, please give me a call after you come back.)

_____

E Translate these sentences into Chinese. PRESENTATIONAL

1 Student A: Do you know Miss Chang?

_____

Student B: I don't know her.

_____

Student A: This is a photo of Miss Chang.

_____

Student B: She is tall and pretty. I'd like to meet her.

_____

Student A: No problem. I'll call her now.

_____

Student B: Great!

_____

2 Student A: I have a meeting tomorrow. Help me prepare, okay?

_____

Student B: Sure, I will help you after dinner. Could you wait a bit?

_____

Student A: Okay, I'll wait for you.

_____

3 Student A: When are you free today?

_____

Student B: I have three classes today, and won't be free until after 2:30 p.m. What's the matter?

_____

Student A: I'd like to ask you to practice Chinese with me.

_____

Student B: Okay, I'll wait for you at the library at 3:00 p.m.

_____

F Write an email to your classmate to see if he/she can practice Chinese with you tomorrow evening. Promise your classmate that you will buy him/her a cup of coffee afterwards. PRESENTATIONAL

_____

_____

_____

G Plan a perfect date. Indicate where and when you wish to meet with your date, and list what you would like to do by using the sentence pattern "A 跟 B + V(O)." PRESENTATIONAL

_____

_____

_____

Lesson 7

第七课

学中文
Studying Chinese

 Check off the following items as you learn them.

Useful Expressions

[ ] Good morning.

[ ] How about it?

[ ] That would be great!

[ ] I'm flattered.

[ ] That's so cool.

Cultural Norms

[ ] Accepting compliments

[ ] Character-writing systems

[ ] Traditional writing instruments

[ ] Value placed on education

As you progress through the lesson, note other useful expressions and cultural norms you would like to learn.

_____

_____

_____

Dialogue 1:
How Did You Do on the Exam?

Audio

Listening Comprehension

A Listen to the Textbook Dialogue 1 audio, then mark these statements true or false. INTERPRETIVE

1 _____ Li You didn't do well on her test last week.

2 _____ Wang Peng writes Chinese characters well, but very slowly.

3 _____ Wang Peng didn't want to teach Li You how to write Chinese characters.

4 _____ Li You has gone over tomorrow's lesson.

5 _____ The Chinese characters in Lesson 7 are very easy.

6 _____ Li You has no problems with Lesson 7's grammar.

B Listen to the Workbook Narrative audio, then mark these statements true or false. INTERPRETIVE

1 _____ Mr. Li likes studying Chinese, but not English.

2 _____ Mr. Li feels that English grammar is not too difficult, but Chinese grammar is hard.

3 _____ Mr. Li has some difficulty with Chinese characters.

C Listen to the Workbook Dialogue audio, then mark these statements true or false. INTERPRETIVE

1 _____ The woman didn't do very well on the Chinese test last week.

2 _____ The woman confessed that she spent a lot of time watching TV.

3 _____ The man thinks that the woman should have been more prepared.

4 _____ The woman thinks that the man was too busy to help her.

A Identify the characters with the same initials (either *zh* or *x*) and write them in *pinyin*.

学 习 枝 纸 写 张 真

1 *zh:* _____

2 *x:* _____

B Compare the tones of these characters. Indicate the tones with 1 (first tone), 2 (second tone), 3 (third tone), 4 (fourth tone), or 0 (neutral tone).

1 纸 _____ 只 _____

2 字 _____ 子 _____

3 难 _____ 男 _____

Speaking

A Answer these questions in Chinese based on Textbook Dialogue 1. PRESENTATIONAL

1 How did Li You do on last week's test? Why?

2 Why does Wang Peng offer to help Li You with her writing of Chinese characters?

3 Who writes Chinese characters quickly?

4 Which lesson will Li You study tomorrow?

5 How does Li You feel about the grammar, vocabulary, and characters in the lesson she has prepared?

6 What will Wang Peng and Li You do tonight?

B Comment on the grammar, vocabulary, and characters in the last lesson you studied.
PRESENTATIONAL

C In pairs, discuss the result of your recent Chinese test. Comment on how you did in learning the grammar, reviewing the vocabulary, and writing the characters. INTERPERSONAL

A Read this note that Little Bai left for Little Wang, then mark the statements true or false. INTERPRETIVE

小王：

你好！我上个星期有个中文考试，我考得不太好。我写汉字写得不错，可是太慢。中文语法也有一点儿难，我不太懂。这个周末你有时间吗？我想请你帮我复习中文。好吗？

小白

1 _____ Little Bai did well on the exam.

2 _____ Little Bai wrote the characters pretty well, although slowly.

3 _____ Little Bai didn't understand the grammar at all.

4 _____ Little Bai hoped to see Little Wang this afternoon.

5 _____ Little Wang's Chinese seems to be better than Little Bai's.

B Read this passage written by a student, then mark the statements true or false. INTERPRETIVE

我们都不喜欢考试，但是我们的中文老师常常给我们考试。我们喜欢唱歌、跳舞，可是我们的老师不唱歌，也不跳舞，很没有意思。她说我们得常常听中文、练习说中文。要是我们听了、练习了，她就很高兴。要是我们没听、没练习，她就很不高兴。有的时候，我们还得去她的办公室请她帮我们复习。要是老师不来学校上课，不给我们考试，在家喝茶、看电视、聊天，那不是很好吗？

1 _____ The narrator considers her attitude toward tests representative of her fellow students.

2 _____ The teacher is popular because she and the students have similar hobbies.

3 _____ The teacher seems to care a lot about her students' education.

4 _____ The students often have tea with the teacher in her office.

5 _____ The teacher has decided not to give tests to the students anymore.

6 _____ The narrator hopes the teacher will invite the students to visit her home.

C Read this passage, then mark the statements true or false. INTERPRETIVE

昨天是小高的生日，李友和王朋都到小高家去了。他们一起喝茶、听音乐、唱歌，晚上十二点才回家。王朋因为喝了很多茶，所以睡觉睡得不好。李友因为昨天没有准备，所以今天考试考得不好。

1 _____ Both Wang Peng and Li You went to Little Gao's place.

2 _____ Wang Peng, Li You, and Little Gao were out yesterday evening.

3 _____ Wang Peng was the only one who drank tea last night.

4 _____ Wang Peng didn't sleep well last night because he had too much cola.

5 _____ Li You didn't have time yesterday to prepare for today's test.

D Would you be interested in reading this book? Why or why not? INTERPRETIVE

Writing and Grammar

A Write the *pinyin* for the characters in the top row, compare them with the *pinyin* of the characters below, then consider the relationship between each pair.

1 字 _____   2 慢 _____   3 枝 _____

子 *(zǐ)*   曼 *(màn)*   支 *(zhī)*

4 懂 _____   5 张 _____   6 试 _____

董 *(dǒng)*   长 *(zhǎng)*   式 *(shì)*

B Draw a line connecting the object with its proper measure word. PRESENTATIONAL

1   一位

2    一杯

3   一瓶

4   一枝

5   一张

C What kinds of praise have you received or would you like to receive from your teacher, friends, or classmates? List them by using 得, following the example below. PRESENTATIONAL

说中文 | 好

你说中文说得很好。

1 打球 | 很好 _____

2 写字 | 漂亮 _____

3 说英文 | 快 _____

4 考试 | 好 _____

5 预习生词语法 | 不错 _____

D Based on the images, write sentences about giving. Follow the example below. PRESENTATIONAL

 给王朋一瓶可乐。

1 _____

2  _____

3   _____

4   _____

E Fill in the blanks with the numbered words. Each word may be used only once. PRESENTATIONAL

1 太   5 一起

2 有一点儿   6 常常

3 都   7 可是

4 也

我和我的姐姐_____喜欢听音乐。我们_____ _____听。我们_____喜欢学中文。_____中国人说中文说得_____快。我觉得语法也_____难。

F Which of these tasks are urgent enough that you think you should do them right away? Select four to make sentences, following the example below. PRESENTATIONAL

a 去同学家玩儿   f 练习说中文

b 跟男／女朋友见面   g 练习写汉字

c 跟妈妈说话   h 准备考试

d 回家睡觉   i 预习生词语法

e 去学校开会

Task: 给爸爸打电话

我<u>现在就</u>给爸爸打电话。

1 _____

2 _____

3 _____

4 _____

Translate these sentences into Chinese.

1   Student A: I think Chinese is interesting.

_____

    Student B: But I feel that Chinese grammar is a bit hard.

_____

2   Student A: How about you teach me how to write characters?

_____

    Student B: OK, give me a pen. Let's write them now.

_____

3   Student A: How did you do on the test?

_____

    Student B: I reviewed Lesson 6 well, so I did well.

_____

4   Student A: I write Chinese characters way too slowly.

_____

    Student B: I speak Chinese way too slowly.

_____

5   Student A: Could you help me practice speaking Chinese?

_____

    Student B: I speak Chinese poorly. Let's go to the teacher's office and ask the teacher to help us.

_____

    Student A: OK. We'll go find him now.

_____

H Comment on how well or how badly your family, classmates, friends, or any celebrities perform these activities. Follow the example below. PRESENTATIONAL

我觉得林书豪 *(Lín Shūháo)* (Jeremy Lin) 打球打得不错。

1 打球 _____

2 唱歌 _____

3 跳舞 _____

4 工作 _____

5 说英文 _____

6 学中文 _____

7 预习生词语法 _____

8 准备考试 _____

Dialogue 2:
Preparing for Chinese Class

> ## Listening Comprehension

A Listen to the Textbook Dialogue 2 audio, then mark these statements true or false. INTERPRETIVE

1 _____ Bai Ying'ai is always late.

2 _____ Bai Ying'ai didn't go to bed until early this morning.

3 _____ Li You went to bed very late because she was studying Chinese.

4 _____ Li You recited the lesson well because she listened to the audio the night before.

5 _____ According to Bai Ying'ai, Li You has a very handsome Chinese friend.

B Listen to the Workbook Dialogue audio, then mark these statements true or false. INTERPRETIVE

1 _____ The man usually comes early.

2 _____ The man previewed Lesson 8.

3 _____ The man went to bed early because he didn't have homework last night.

4 _____ The man usually goes to bed around 9:00 p.m.

> ## Pinyin and Tone

A Identify the characters with the same finals (either *an* or *ang*) and write them in *pinyin*.

晚　上　慢　张　汉　难

1 *an:* _____

2 *ang:* _____

B Compare the tones of these characters. Indicate the tones with 1 (first tone), 2 (second tone), 3 (third tone), 4 (fourth tone), or 0 (neutral tone).

1 喜 _____ 习 _____　　3 工 _____ 功 _____

2 纸 _____ 枝 _____　　4 语 _____ 预 _____

A Answer these questions in Chinese based on Textbook Dialogue 2. PRESENTATIONAL

1 Why did Bai Ying'ai come so late today?

2 Why was Li You able to go to bed early last night?

3 Why did Bai Ying'ai say that it is nice to have a Chinese friend?

4 Which lesson is the class studying today?

5 Who did not listen to the audio last night?

6 How did Bai Ying'ai describe Li You's friend?

B In pairs, have a conversation about scheduling. Find out if your partner was early or late for class, went to bed early or late, and prepared for today's lesson or not. INTERPERSONAL

Reading Comprehension

A Read Li You's schedule for today, then mark the statements true or false. INTERPRETIVE

上午	八点半	预习生词
	九点一刻	听录音
	十点	上中文课
中午	十二点	吃午饭
下午	一点	睡觉
	两点	复习中文
晚上	六点	吃晚饭
	八点	做功课

1 _____ 李友今天没有课。

2 _____ 李友上午预习生词。

3 _____ 李友下午听录音。

4 _____ 李友不吃午饭，只吃晚饭。

5 _____ 李友复习中文以后睡午觉。

6 _____ 李友吃晚饭以后做功课。

Read this passage, then mark the statements true or false. INTERPRETIVE

今天上午，小李预习了第六课。第六课的语法有点儿难，生词也很多。下午她要去老师的办公室问问题。她觉得学中文很有意思，说中国话不太难，可是汉字有一点儿难。

1 ____ Little Li thinks Lesson 6 is hard.

2 ____ Little Li will go to her teacher's office today.

3 ____ Little Li's teacher will give her a test this afternoon.

4 ____ Little Li feels very frustrated with her Chinese.

5 ____ Little Li considers speaking Chinese easier than writing Chinese characters.

C Read this passage, then answer the questions by circling the most appropriate choice. INTERPRETIVE

小美是中国学生，在美国大学学英文。昨天下午她在图书馆做功课。她觉得英文生词太多，语法也不容易。因为一个美国男学生帮她复习生词和语法，所以她做功课做得很快。那个美国男生很帅，很酷。今天小美想给他打电话，才知道没有问他的名字和电话。

1 Which of these statements about Xiaomei is true?

   a She is a Chinese student tutoring American students in Chinese.

   b She is an American student taking a Chinese class.

   c She is a Chinese student taking an English class.

   d She is an American student studying Chinese with Chinese students.

2 Which of these statements is true about her homework yesterday?

   a She completed it quickly because the grammar and vocabulary were easy.

   b She completed it quickly even though the grammar and vocabulary were difficult.

   c She completed it slowly because the grammar and vocabulary were difficult.

   d She completed it slowly even though the grammar and vocabulary were easy.

D Based on the passage from (C), mark these statements true or false. INTERPRETIVE

1 ____ We can assume that Xiaomei likes the young man she met.

2 ____ Xiaomei had the young man's phone number.

E How many of these books are about Chinese grammar and how many are about Chinese characters? INTERPRETIVE

Writing and Grammar

A Write the common radical and the characters, then compound each character with another one to form a disyllabic word that you have learned (write the common radicals in 1 and 5).

这　还　进

1

2 ____

3 ____

4 ____

话 课 词 语

5 ☐ _____   8 ☐ _____

6 ☐ _____   9 ☐ _____

7 ☐ _____

B When people give praise or make complaints, they often use 真 or 太. Fill in the blanks with the appropriate word. PRESENTATIONAL

1 老师说话说得＿＿＿慢了，学生都不想听。

2 功课＿＿＿多，晚上得听录音、写汉字。

3 早上七点半就得去学校上课，＿＿＿早了。

4 你哥哥＿＿＿帅，很多女孩子都想认识他。

5 小王写汉字写得＿＿＿漂亮，我想请他教我怎么写。

6 你念课文念得＿＿＿不错，常常听录音吧？

7 李老师上课上得＿＿＿好了，大家都喜欢上他的课。

Answer these questions according to your own circumstances, following the example below. INTERPERSONAL

Q: 你昨天睡觉睡得晚吗？

A: 我睡觉睡得很晚／不晚。

1 Q: 你写字写得快吗？

A: _____

2 Q: 你唱歌唱得好吗？

A: _____

3 Q: 你打球打得好吗？

A: _____

4 Q: 你跳舞跳得怎么样？

A: _____

5 Q: 你念课文念得怎么样？

A: _____

D Last week Little Li was either late or early. Complete these sentences with either 才 or 就, following the example below. PRESENTATIONAL

学校下午三点开会。　　　　　　　2:00 p.m.

学校下午三点开会，小李两点就来了。

1 我们昨天上午九点钟考试。　　　　8:45 a.m.

_____

2 我们星期一去老师办公室问问题。　Wednesday

_____

3 我们星期四预习生词语法。 Tuesday

_____

4 我们昨天晚上十点回家。 11:30 p.m.

_____

E Translate these sentences into Chinese. PRESENTATIONAL

1 Student A: How come you have so much homework tonight?

_____

Student B: The teacher is going to give us a test tomorrow, and I have to review the text and practice writing Chinese.

_____

_____

2 Student A: Did you prepare Lesson 8 last night?

_____

Student B: No, I didn't. I went to bed early at 9:30.

_____

Student A: That was indeed early. I didn't go to bed until 1:30.

_____

Student B: That's way too late.

_____

3 Student A: This is my boyfriend's picture.

_____

Student B: He is very handsome.

_____

Student A: He sings well, dances well, and plays ball well.

_____

Student B: That's so cool!

_____

F Is there a famous person you admire? List your idols and describe their appeal, following the example below. PRESENTATIONAL

林书豪 *(Lín Shūháo)* (Jeremy Lin) 真酷，他打球打得真好。

_____

_____

_____

_____

G Translate this passage into Chinese. PRESENTATIONAL

My younger sister did not learn Chinese well. She didn't like listening to the audio and didn't practice speaking, so she did not speak well. She didn't like studying grammar or writing characters. That was why she didn't do well on the exams. But after she met a Chinese friend, they often reviewed Chinese together in the library. Now, she likes listening to the audio and she also writes characters pretty well.

_____

_____

_____

_____

_____

学校生活

School Life

 Check off the following items as you learn them.

Useful Expressions

[ ] How are things recently?

[ ] What time are we going?

[ ] I hope you can come.

[ ] Please don't poke fun at me.

[ ] Wishing you all the best.

Cultural Norms

[ ] College entrance exams

[ ] School schedules

[ ] Formal writing conventions

As you progress through the lesson, note other useful expressions and cultural norms you would like to learn.

_____

_____

_____

Diary Entry: A Typical School Day

Audio

Listening Comprehension

A Listen to the Textbook Diary Entry audio, then circle the most appropriate choice. INTERPRETIVE

1 What did Li You do this morning before breakfast?

 a She took a bath.

 b She listened to the audio.

 c She checked her email.

 d She talked to her friend on the phone.

2 What time did Li You go to class this morning?

 a 7:30

 b 8:00

 c 8:30

 d 9:00

3 What did Li You not do in her Chinese class?

 a take a test

 b practice pronunciation

 c learn vocabulary

 d study grammar

4 Where did Li You have lunch today?

 a at a Chinese restaurant

 b at the school cafeteria

 c at home

 d at her friend's house

5 What was Li You doing around 4:30 p.m.?

 a practicing Chinese

 b checking her email

 c playing ball

 d drinking coffee

6 What time did Li You eat dinner?

 a 5:45

 b 6:00

 c 6:30

 d 7:30

7 Why did Li You visit Bai Ying'ai's dorm?

 a to eat dinner

 b to play video games

 c to chat

 d to study

8 What time did Li You return to her place?

 a 7:30

 b 8:30

 c 9:30

 d 10:30

9 What did Li You do before she went to bed?

 a visit Little Bai

 b finish her homework

 c talk to Gao Wenzhong on the phone

 d study for her test

B Listen to the Textbook Diary Entry audio, then number the images in the correct sequence.

1

    _____

2

    _____

3

    _____

C Listen to the Workbook Dialogue audio, then mark these statements true or false. INTERPRETIVE

1 ____ Li You is going to Teacher Zhang's office at 4:00 p.m. today.

2 ____ Wang Peng will be attending a class at 2:30 p.m. today.

3 ____ Li You plans to do research at the library this evening.

4 ____ Li You and Wang Peng will see each other in the library this evening.

Pinyin and Tone

A Identify the characters with the same initials (either *j* or *q*) and write them in *pinyin*.

记 起 前 经 教 请

1 *j:* _____

2 *q:* _____

B Compare the tones of these characters. Indicate the tones with 1 (first tone), 2 (second tone), 3 (third tone), 4 (fourth tone), or 0 (neutral tone).

1 哪 _____ 那 _____   4 宿 _____ 诉 _____

2 早 _____ 澡 _____   5 高 _____ 告 _____

3 到 _____ 道 _____   6 知 _____ 纸 _____

A Answer these questions in Chinese based on the Textbook Diary Entry. PRESENTATIONAL

1 What did Li You do after getting up?

2 Did Li You have breakfast?

3 How many classes did Li You have?

4 What did the teacher do in Li You's first class?

5 What did Li You do during her lunch hour?

6 What did Li You do at the library?

7 What did Li You do after dinner?

B In pairs, review this schedule and take turns describing what Wang Peng did yesterday morning.
INTERPERSONAL

Reading Comprehension

A Read this schedule for Little Wang, then mark the statements true or false. INTERPRETIVE

8:00 a.m.	复习第七课生词、语法
9:00 a.m.	上电脑课
10:00 a.m.	去常老师的办公室练习发音
2:30 p.m.	去图书馆看书
4:00 p.m.	去打球
6:00 p.m.	去宿舍餐厅吃晚饭
8:15 p.m.	给小李打电话，跟他一起练习中文
10:30 p.m.	给爸爸妈妈打电话
12:00 a.m.	睡觉

1 _____ 小王今天只有一节课。

2 _____ 小王跟小白一起吃午饭。

3 _____ 小王上午去找常老师。

4 _____ 小王去小李家练习中文。

5 _____ 小王吃晚饭以前去打球。

6 _____ 小王去图书馆以后去找常老师。

7 _____ 小王睡觉以前给爸爸妈妈打电话。

8 _____ 小王跟小李练习中文以后才吃饭。

B Read this passage, then mark the statements true or false. INTERPRETIVE

小高以前常常跟朋友一起打球、聊天、看电视，不做功课。可是因为他下星期要考试，所以这个星期他不打球、不看电视、也不找朋友聊天，一个人到图书馆去看书。他很早就起床，很晚才睡觉，所以他上课的时候常常想睡觉。

1 _____ 小高以前常常跟朋友一边做功课，
　　　　一边聊天。

2 _____ 小高常常跟朋友一起到图书馆去看书。

3 _____ 因为小高要准备考试，所以他这个
　　　　星期只看书，不玩儿。

4 _____ 小高觉得上课没有意思，所以他上课
　　　　的时候常常想睡觉。

5 _____ 这个星期小高睡觉睡得很早。

小李： 你认识小常的男朋友文书明吗？

小白： 我认识。昨天我去图书馆上网的时候，他正在跟小常一起做功课。

小李： 我也认识他，因为他跟我一起上电脑课。

小白： 我觉得他很酷！

小李： 他很帅，可是我不太喜欢他。

小白： 是吗？为什么？

小李： 别人说他有的时候一边给小常打电话，一边上网跟别的女孩子聊天。

小白： 是吗？小常知道不知道？你得告诉她！

1 ＿＿ Little Bai is Little Chang's friend, but Little Li is not.

2 ＿＿ Little Bai is in the same computer class as Wen Shuming.

3 ＿＿ Little Chang and Wen Shuming did their homework together yesterday.

4 ＿＿ Little Bai saw Little Li in the library yesterday.

5 ＿＿ Little Li thinks Wen Shuming is handsome, but does not like him.

6 ＿＿ At the end of the dialogue, Little Bai wants Little Li to talk to Little Chang.

Writing and Grammar

A These characters all share the same radical, 纟. Compound each of them with another character to form a disyllabic word, then write the meaning of the word in English.

1 经 _____ _____

2 约 _____ _____

3 练 _____ _____

4 绍 _____ _____

B Wang Peng is multi-talented and a good friend. Based on the images, state what he can teach his friends. Follow the example below. **PRESENTATIONAL**

中 王朋教朋友写汉字。

1 _____

2 _____

3 _____

4 _____

C Nowadays, people often multitask. Based on the images, describe what these people are doing. Follow the example below. PRESENTATIONAL

 他一边儿吃早饭，一边儿看电视。

1  _____

2 _____

3  _____

4  _____

D Based on the images, describe what these people are doing. Follow the example below. PRESENTATIONAL

 他正在上课。

1 _____

2 _____

3  _____

4 _____

5 _____

E Translate these sentences into Chinese. PRESENTATIONAL

1 Student A: What do you want to do after class?

_____

Student B: I want to go back to the dorm to do homework.

_____

2 Student A: You speak Chinese so well. Could you help me practice before tomorrow's test?

_____

Student B: No problem. Let's have coffee and practice at the same time.

_____

3 Student A: This new text is a bit difficult.

_____

Student B: Let's ask the teacher when we meet her tomorrow.

_____

4 Student A: I'll go to the cafeteria to have lunch right after the test. Have you had lunch already?

_____

Student B: Don't wait for me. I have to work. I don't know when I'll have lunch today.

_____

F You are a newly hired personal assistant and your partner is your boss. Find out the following information so you can plan his/her schedule. INTERPERSONAL

1 When your boss gets up in the morning.

2 Whether your boss prefers to have breakfast at home or in the office.

3 When and with whom your boss has regular meetings.

4 What time your boss has lunch and dinner.

5 What time your boss plans to return home after work.

6 What time your boss goes to bed.

7 Any other daily activities that should be included in the schedule.

G After gathering your boss's information, you now need to enter it in your phone. PRESENTATIONAL

1 _____

2 _____

3 _____

4 _____

5 _____

6 _____

7 _____

H Describe your daily routine. PRESENTATIONAL

_____

_____

_____

_____

Letter: Writing to a Friend

Listening Comprehension

A Listen to the Textbook Letter audio, then mark these statements true or false. INTERPRETIVE

1 _____ This is a letter from Li You to Wang Peng.

2 _____ Li You's major is Chinese.

3 _____ Li You does not like her Chinese class at all.

4 _____ Li You's Chinese teacher speaks English very well.

5 _____ Li You is learning Chinese quickly because she has some help.

6 _____ Li You would like her friend to attend her school concert.

B Listen to the Workbook Narrative 1 audio, then mark these statements true or false. INTERPRETIVE

1 _____ Wang Peng went to the library to help Li You with her Chinese.

2 _____ Wang Peng did not go to play ball this afternoon until he had finished his homework.

3 _____ Li You went to a movie with Wang Peng this evening.

4 _____ Li You has a Chinese class tomorrow.

C Listen to the Workbook Narrative 2 audio that describes Little Li's activities yesterday, then place the letters representing those activities in the column to the right. INTERPRETIVE

a

b

c

d

1 _____

2 _____

3 _____

4 _____

e

5 _____

f

6 _____

g

7 _____

h

8 _____

Pinyin and Tone

A Identify the characters with the same initials (either *j* or *zh*) and write them in *pinyin*.

祝　教　知　近　就　专　节

1 *j:* _____

2 *zh:* _____

B Compare the tones of these characters. Indicate the tones with 1 (first tone), 2 (second tone), 3 (third tone), 4 (fourth tone), or 0 (neutral tone).

1 希 _____ 洗 _____   4 笑 _____ 小 _____

2 新 _____ 信 _____   5 网 _____ 望 _____

3 也 _____ 业 _____   6 医 _____ 以 _____

A Answer these questions in Chinese based on the Textbook Letter. PRESENTATIONAL

1 Why is Li You so busy this semester?

2 Describe Li You's Chinese class.

3 How did Li You feel about her Chinese class? Why?

4 Why did Li You ask Xiaoyin if she liked music?

B Describe your Chinese class to your friends in great detail. Make sure to comment on pronunciation, grammar, vocabulary, and Chinese characters. PRESENTATIONAL

Reading Comprehension

A Read this email, then answer the questions by circling the most appropriate choice. INTERPRETIVE

文书明：

你好！谢谢你那天在图书馆帮我复习英文语法。我的英文不好，请你别笑我。那天我不知道你的名字，但是后来我的朋友告诉我，你有一个漂亮的中文名字。我还知道，你这个学期除了电脑专业课以外，还在学中文。这个周末有一个中国电影，希望你能来看。有空的时候给我打个电话，好吗？我的电话是555-5555。

小美

1 How does Xiaomei feel about her English?
  a frustrated
  b embarrassed
  c proud

2 Where did Xiaomei get her information about Wen Shuming?

    a   from Wen Shuming himself

    b   from the librarian

    c   from a friend

3 According to Xiaomei, which of the following facts about Wen Shuming is correct?

    a   He is a computer science major who studies Chinese.

    b   He is a Chinese major who studies computer science.

    c   He is a student who majors in Chinese and computer science.

4 What does Xiaomei hope Wen Shuming will do?

    a   come to see the movie but not call her

    b   call her but not come to the movie

    c   call her and come to the movie

B Read this passage, then mark the statements true or false. **INTERPRETIVE**

小高今天很忙，上午除了有三节课以外，还有一个电脑考试。他中午跟朋友一起吃饭，下午在图书馆看书、做功课，晚上在电脑室上网聊天儿，十点才回家吃晚饭。晚饭以后，他一边看电视，一边预习明天的功课，十二点半才睡觉。

1 _____ 小高上午没空。

2 _____ 小高下午不在家，在图书馆工作。

3 _____ 小高晚上很晚才吃饭。

4 _____ 小高晚上在电脑室预习明天的功课。

5 _____ 小高一边听音乐，一边看书。

C Read this passage, then list five ways in which you are similar to or different from the narrator. Write your statements in English, starting with "Like the person" or "Unlike the person." INTERPRETIVE

> 我是大学一年级的学生。开始我不知道教室在哪儿，因为学校太大了；我不喜欢吃学校餐厅的饭，因为餐厅的饭太不好吃了；我也不会用学校图书馆的电脑，因为图书馆的电脑太新了；在宿舍洗澡也很不方便。中文课很难。除了生词太多以外，我还觉得老师说话说得太快。

1 _____

2 _____

3 _____

4 _____

5 _____

Writing and Grammar

A You have just learned the character 用, which has the semi-enclosing pattern. Write three more characters in the same pattern, compound each of them with another character to form a disyllabic word, then translate the word into English.

Semi - Enclosing

1 ☐ _____ _____   3 ☐ _____ _____

2 ☐ _____ _____

1 一 ＿＿＿＿＿ 老师　　　6 一 ＿＿＿＿＿ 可乐

2 一 ＿＿＿＿＿ 照片　　　7 一 ＿＿＿＿＿ 课

3 一 ＿＿＿＿＿ 电脑　　　8 一 ＿＿＿＿＿ 课文

4 一 ＿＿＿＿＿ 笔　　　　9 一 ＿＿＿＿＿ 信

5 一 ＿＿＿＿＿ 咖啡　　　10 我家有三 ＿＿＿＿＿ 人。

C Answer these questions involving tools, methods, or means. Follow the example below.
INTERPERSONAL

Q: 高文中用什么做功课？

A: 他用电脑做功课。

1 Q: 白英爱怎么学发音？

A: ＿＿＿＿＿＿＿＿＿＿＿＿＿＿＿＿＿＿＿

2 Q: 李友用什么练习写汉字？

A: ＿＿＿＿＿＿＿＿＿＿＿＿＿＿＿＿＿＿＿

3 Q: 高小音用中文还是英文写信？

A: ＿＿＿＿＿＿＿＿＿＿＿＿＿＿＿＿＿＿＿

D Based on the images, list some of the things that Bai Ying'ai can do, and the one thing she cannot do. Follow the example below. PRESENTATIONAL

✓ 她会写英文。

1 　✓ ＿＿＿＿＿＿＿＿＿＿＿＿＿＿

2  ✓ _____

3  ✓ _____

4  ✗ _____

E Based on the images, list some activities that are typically forbidden at home or in class. Follow the example below. PRESENTATIONAL

老师告诉我，考试的时候，✗ 。

老师告诉我，考试的时候，<u>不能问问题</u>。

1 老师告诉我，上课的时候，✗ 。

_____

2 老师告诉我，上课的时候，✗ 。

_____

3 妈妈告诉我，做功课的时候，✗ 。

_____

4 妈妈告诉我，吃饭的时候，✗ 。

_____

F Describe what each person does or can do using "除了…以外，还…" Follow the example below. PRESENTATIONAL

高文中除了喜欢唱歌以外，还喜欢跳舞。

1

_____

2

_____

3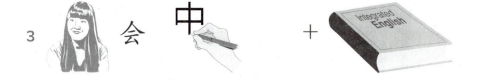

_____

G Translate these sentences into Chinese. PRESENTATIONAL

1 **Student A:** What are you doing?

_____

Student B: I am writing a letter to my friend.

_____

Student A: Really? Are you writing it in English or Chinese?

_____

Student B: I'm writing it in Chinese. She doesn't know English.

_____

2   **Student A:**   Did Teacher Chang help you practice speaking Chinese yesterday?

_____

      Student B: No. She was at a meeting when I got to her office.

_____

3   **Student A:**   What's your major?

_____

      Student B: My major is Chinese.

_____

      Student A: Great! Can you teach me Chinese characters?

_____

      Student B: OK, I'll help you right after my class.

_____

4   **Student A:**   You write characters so quickly.

_____

      Student B: At first, I wrote very slowly. But later, my oldest brother helped me practice. Now I write quickly.

_____

5   **Student A:**   Tomorrow is the weekend. I hope you can go to a concert with me.

_____

      Student B: I'm sorry. I can't go. I have to work.

_____

6   **Student A:**   This grammar is a bit difficult. Do you understand it?

_____

      Student B: Don't ask me, I don't understand it either.

_____

Based on the images, write down what Little Wang did yesterday. PRESENTATIONAL

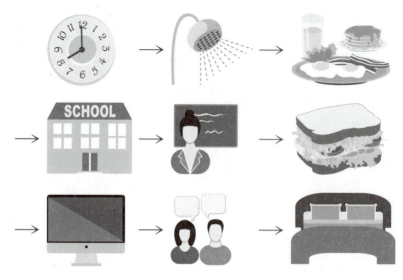

小王的一天

_____

_____

_____

_____

_____

Write your friend an email in Chinese. Tell him/her about your experience learning Chinese. Include information about your study habits, in-class situation, after-class work, strengths and weaknesses, and likes and dislikes. Also comment on how your instructor teaches or how your classmates study. Don't forget to ask your friend about his/her studies, and wish him/her the best. PRESENTATIONAL

_____

_____

_____

_____

买东西
Shopping

 Check off the following items as you learn them.

Useful Expressions

[ ] I'd like to buy a pair of shoes.

[ ] What color do you like?

[ ] What size?

[ ] I'll take them.

[ ] Can I use my credit card here?

Cultural Norms

[ ] Shopping etiquette

[ ] Popular e-commerce sites

[ ] Traditional clothing types

[ ] Denominations of currency

As you progress through the lesson, note other useful expressions and cultural norms you would like to learn.

_____

_____

_____

Dialogue 1: Shopping for Clothes

Audio

Listening Comprehension

A Listen to the Textbook Dialogue 1 audio, then circle the most appropriate choice. INTERPRETIVE

1 What color shirt does Li You want to buy?

  a black

  b white

  c red

  d yellow

2 What else does Li You want to buy besides the shirt?

  a a hat

  b a pair of shoes

  c a sweater

  d a pair of pants

3 What size does Li You wear?

  a small

  b medium

  c large

  d extra large

4 How much does Li You need to pay altogether?

  a between $20 and $30

  b between $30 and $40

  c between $40 and $50

  d between $50 and $60

B Listen to the Workbook Narrative audio, then circle the most appropriate choice. INTERPRETIVE

1 What color does Wang Peng like?

  a blue

  b brown

  c white

  d red

2 Why doesn't Wang Peng like the shirt?

  a It's too expensive.

  b It's not stylish.

  c He doesn't like the color.

  d It doesn't fit.

3 What colors did the salesperson say they had?

   a   white, blue, and brown

   b   white, red, and brown

   c   red, blue, and white

   d   white, red, and yellow

4 When did Wang Peng buy the shirt?

   a   five days ago

   b   seven days ago

   c   ten days ago

   d   fourteen days ago

Pinyin and Tone

A Identify the characters with the same initials (either *ch* or *sh*) and write them in *pinyin*.

商　长　售　衬　衫　穿

1 *ch:* _____

2 *sh:* _____

B Compare the tones of these characters. Indicate the tones with 1 (first tone), 2 (second tone), 3 (third tone), 4 (fourth tone), or 0 (neutral tone).

1 衣 _____ 宜 _____ 　　4 商 _____ 上 _____

2 件 _____ 间 _____ 　　5 合 _____ 喝 _____

3 裤 _____ 酷 _____ 　　6 店 _____ 点 _____

A Answer these questions in Chinese based on Textbook Dialogue 1. PRESENTATIONAL

1 What does Li You want to buy?

2 What color does Li You like?

3 What does Li You like about the pants?

4 Give the price for each item, and the total cost.

B In pairs, ask each other what size clothing you wear, what color you prefer, and the price of the clothing you are wearing. INTERPERSONAL

Reading Comprehension

A Read this passage, then mark the statements true or false. INTERPRETIVE

小文上个周末去买东西。他想买一件中号的红衬衫，可是中号衬衫都是白的，红衬衫都是大号的。售货员很客气，她帮小文找了一件衬衫，不是红的，可是颜色不错。那位售货员告诉他，这件衬衫三十九块九毛九。小文觉得有一点儿贵，可是他觉得要是不买就对不起那位售货员，所以给了售货员四十块钱买了那件衬衫。

1 _____ There were many items in the store for Little Wen to choose from.

2 _____ The salesperson was very courteous.

3 _____ Little Wen probably wears a size medium shirt.

4 _____ Little Wen was looking for a white shirt.

5 _____ The salesperson finally found a red shirt that Little Wen liked.

6 _____ Little Wen bought the shirt because he didn't want to disappoint the salesperson.

B Read this dialogue, then mark the statements true or false. INTERPRETIVE

男：我今天买了一件衬衫，你看怎么样？

女：大小很合适，可是颜色不太好。你喜欢穿红衬衫，怎么买了这个颜色的？

男：我想买红的，可是红衬衫都太大了。

女：那你为什么买这件？

男：因为那位售货员……

女：很漂亮，对不对？

男：不，不，不。她不认识我，但是我知道她是你的朋友。

女：是吗？

1 ____ The woman likes the color but not the size of the man's new shirt.

2 ____ The woman is somewhat surprised that the man bought that shirt.

3 ____ We can assume that many of the man's shirts are red.

4 ____ The man bought the shirt because the price was right.

5 ____ The salesperson turns out to be the man's friend.

C According to this index from a newspaper's classified section, on what page can you find ads for apparel? INTERPRETIVE

专项分类资讯 ▶ ▶ ▶			
二手房超市、租房手册		音像软件	79版
	36版	家居建材	81版
美好姻缘	54版	健康专递	82版
招生广场	66、69版	服装服饰	82版
美容美发招生	67版	五金、机械、化工	83版
择业直通车	70、71版	印刷设计	83版
留学与移民	72版	快乐京郊游	84版
汽车服务	75版	天天美容	84版

A Which of these characters are based on the top-bottom pattern, and which on the left-right pattern? After filling in the answers, write the characters in the spaces provided.

Top - Bottom	Left - Right
a	**b**

1 ___ 服

2 ___ 件

3 ___ 红

4 ___ 黄

5 ___ 便

6 ___ 宜

7 ___ 短

8 ___ 员

B Based on the images, form question-and-answers about how much different items cost in your city. Follow the example below. PRESENTATIONAL

Q: 一瓶可乐多少钱？

A: 一瓶可乐两块九毛九分钱。

1  _____

2 _____

3 _____

4 _____

5 _____

C Based on the images, form question-and-answers about which items the IC characters prefer. Follow the example below. INTERPERSONAL

Q: 李友喜欢哪（一）件衣服？

A: 她喜欢白（色）的。

1 Q: 王朋要买哪（一）条裤子？

A: _____

2 Q: 高小音想喝哪杯茶？

A: _____

3 Q: 白英爱用哪枝笔？

A: _____

D Translate these sentences into Chinese. PRESENTATIONAL

1 Student A: This shirt is so pretty. Try it on.

_____

Student B: There's no need to. It's too expensive.

_____

2 Student A: What size pants do you wear?

_____

Student B: I wear size 30.

_____

3 Student A: Both the color and the length of the pants are right for you. Get them!

_____

Student B: I'll buy them if they are cheap.

_____

4 Student A: Miss, excuse me, how much is this medium-size shirt?

_____

Student B: It's twenty-nine dollars and fifty cents.

_____

Student A: Here's thirty dollars.

_____

Student B: Here's your change, fifty cents. Thank you.

_____

E Search the online catalog of a local clothing store. List the items you like. Include their colors, sizes, and prices. Bring a printout of the list and describe the items to the class. PRESENTATIONAL

_____

_____

_____

F Describe the clothes you're wearing, including their colors and sizes. PRESENTATIONAL

_____

_____

_____

Dialogue 2: Exchanging Shoes

Listening Comprehension

A Listen to the Textbook Dialogue 2 audio, then circle the most appropriate choice. INTERPRETIVE

1 Why does Wang Peng want to exchange the shoes?
   a The shoes do not fit well.
   b The shoes are damaged.
   c He does not like the price.
   d He does not like the color.

2 What color does Wang Peng prefer?
   a black
   b white
   c brown
   d red

3 In what way is the new pair of shoes like the old pair?
   a They are the same size.
   b They are the same color.
   c They are the same price.
   d They have the same design.

B Listen to the Workbook Dialogue 1 audio, then mark these statements true or false. INTERPRETIVE

1 _____ The man wants to return a shirt for a different one, because he doesn't like the color.

2 _____ The man finally takes a yellow shirt because he likes the color.

3 _____ All the large shirts in the store are yellow.

4 _____ A large shirt would fit the man well.

C Listen to the Workbook Dialogue 2 audio, then mark these statements true or false. INTERPRETIVE

1 _____ The store only sells clothes.

2 _____ The man knows what color and what size to get.

3 _____ The man seeks advice from the salesperson.

4 _____ The man wants to buy the most expensive shirt in the store.

5 _____ The man does not want to ruin the surprise for his girlfriend.

6 _____ The salesperson agrees with the man's choice.

A Identify the characters with the same finals (either *ou* or *uo*) and write them in *pinyin*.

都　多　说　售　货　后　果

1 *ou:* _____

2 *uo:* _____

B Compare the tones of these characters. Indicate the tones with 1 (first tone), 2 (second tone), 3 (third tone), 4 (fourth tone), or 0 (neutral tone).

1 鞋 _____ 谢 _____   4 虽 _____ 岁 _____

2 种 _____ 中 _____   5 付 _____ 服 _____

3 过 _____ 果 _____

Speaking

A Answer these questions in Chinese based on Textbook Dialogue 2. PRESENTATIONAL

1 Why does Wang Peng want to return the shoes for a different pair?

2 Does Wang Peng like the black shoes? Why or why not?

3 What color shoes does Wang Peng finally take? Why?

4 Does Wang Peng pay any additional money for the new shoes? Why or why not?

B Describe the clothes you're wearing today, including their colors, sizes, and prices. PRESENTATIONAL

C In pairs, role-play a dialogue between a salesperson in a clothing store and a customer trying to exchange a shirt that's too large. Make sure that the size, color, and price are all correct. INTERPERSONAL

Reading Comprehension

A Identify the items corresponding to the descriptions on the right. Place the correct letter next to its description.

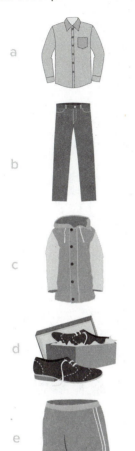

1 短裤 _____

2 长裤 _____

3 大衣 _____

4 衬衫 _____

5 鞋 _____

B Read this passage, then mark the statements true or false. INTERPRETIVE

　　李先生很喜欢买便宜的衣服。所以虽然他的衣服很多，可是他觉得都不太合适。李太太跟她先生不一样。她不喜欢买东西，也不常买东西。李太太只买大小长短和颜色都合适的衣服，所以她的衣服虽然不多，可是她都喜欢。

1 _____ 　李先生觉得买东西很有意思。

2 _____ 　李先生的衣服很多，也都很贵。

3 _____ 李先生的衣服大小和颜色都很合适。

4 _____ 李太太觉得买衣服没意思。

5 _____ 李太太买了很多衣服。

6 _____ 李太太的衣服不大也不小，不长也
不短。

C Look at the sign, identify and circle the goods that are on sale, then explain (in either English or Chinese) what kinds of deals are being offered. INTERPRETIVE

Writing and Grammar

A Write the radical in the character 付 and three characters with the same radical, then provide the meaning of each character in English (write the common radical in 1).

1   3  _____

2 _____   4  _____

B Draw a line from each object to its respective measure word. PRESENTATIONAL

a

b

c

d

e

f

g

h

i

1 位

2 杯

3 瓶

4 封

5 条

6 张

7 双

8 枝

9 件

Answer these questions using "挺···的," following the example below. INTERPERSONAL

Q: 你觉得这一课的生词多不多?

A: 我觉得（这一课的生词）挺多的。

1 Q: 白英爱觉得王朋帅吗?

A: _____

2 Q: 王朋觉得李友漂亮吗?

A: _____

3 Q: 常老师觉得李友念课文念得怎么样?

A: _____

4 Q: 常老师觉得李友写汉字写得怎么样?

A: _____

D Rewrite these sentences using "A 跟 B 一样 + adj," following the example below. PRESENTATIONAL

高文中今年十八岁，李友今年也十八岁。

高文中跟李友一样大。

1 这件衬衫是中号的，那件衬衫也是中号的。

_____

2 这双鞋五十块钱，那双鞋也五十块钱。

_____

3 学中文很酷，学英文也很酷。

_____

4 这个教室很新，那个教室也很新。

_____

5 纽约很有意思，北京也很有意思。

_____

E Based on the information provided, complete this conversation between a salesperson and a customer. PRESENTATIONAL

售货员：_____？

李小姐：我想买一条裤子。

售货员：_____？

李小姐：大号的。

售货员：这条太大了，您可以换 _____。

李小姐：中号的长短、大小都很合适。

售货员：_____？

李小姐：还要买一双鞋。

售货员：_____？

李小姐：黄的。

售货员：一条裤子十九块，一双鞋十五块，
一共 _____。

李小姐：能不能 _____？

售货员：对不起，我们不收 _____ 。

李小姐： _____ 。

售货员：找您六十六块。

F Translate these sentences into Chinese. PRESENTATIONAL

1 **Student A:**   This store is quite nice. Their clothes aren't too expensive.

_____

Student B: Although their clothes aren't too expensive, they don't take credit cards. That's so inconvenient.

_____

_____

2 **Student A:**   What size shirt do you wear?

_____

Student B: I wear medium.

_____

Student A: Do you like this red one? The style and the color are both right (for you).

_____

Student B: I'll try it on.

_____

Student A: It's a little big (on you).

_____

Student B: Let's get a size small.

_____

3 **Student A:** I like to go shopping with my sister. She pays. I don't have to (pay).

_____

_____

Student B: Is that so? Your sister is so nice.

_____

4 **Student A:** I'd like to buy some pens. How much is this kind of pen?

_____

_____

Student B: Three dollars each.

_____

Student A: Why so expensive? How about that kind?

_____

Student B: That kind is as expensive as this kind.

_____

G Write down your comments on a photo of someone that was recently posted on social media. Include details about the fit and color of the clothes he/she is wearing. Indicate whether you like his/her sense of style, and provide some fashion tips. PRESENTATIONAL

_____

_____

_____

_____

H You're shopping for new clothes online. From the items below, choose an outfit. Write a customer review detailing the items you purchased, including their colors, sizes, and prices. Also comment on how you look in your new outfit, how it fits, and if it was too expensive. PRESENTATIONAL

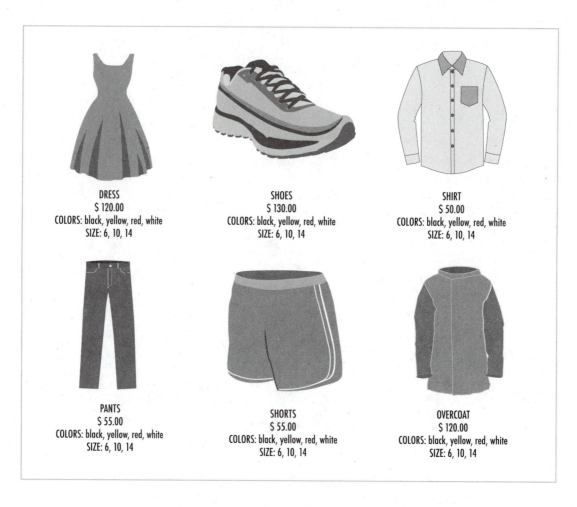

DRESS
$ 120.00
COLORS: black, yellow, red, white
SIZE: 6, 10, 14

SHOES
$ 130.00
COLORS: black, yellow, red, white
SIZE: 6, 10, 14

SHIRT
$ 50.00
COLORS: black, yellow, red, white
SIZE: 6, 10, 14

PANTS
$ 55.00
COLORS: black, yellow, red, white
SIZE: 6, 10, 14

SHORTS
$ 55.00
COLORS: black, yellow, red, white
SIZE: 6, 10, 14

OVERCOAT
$ 120.00
COLORS: black, yellow, red, white
SIZE: 6, 10, 14

_____

_____

_____

_____

_____

交通

Transportation

 Check off the following items as you learn them.

Useful Expressions

[ ] Do you know how to get there?

[ ] Let me drive you home.

[ ] That's too much trouble.

[ ] I'll take the subway.

[ ] Happy New Year!

Cultural Norms

[ ] Modes of transportation

[ ] Popular ridesharing apps

[ ] Common New Year greetings

[ ] Spring Festival traffic

As you progress through the lesson, note other useful expressions and cultural norms you would like to learn.

_____

_____

_____

Dialogue:
Going Home for Winter Vacation

Audio

Listening Comprehension

A Listen to the Textbook Dialogue audio, then mark these statements true or false. INTERPRETIVE

1 _____ Li You will be leaving on the twenty-first.

2 _____ Li You should reach the airport no later than eight o'clock in the morning.

3 _____ Li You decides not to take a taxi because she thinks it is too expensive.

4 _____ Li You doesn't know how to get to the airport by public transportation.

5 _____ To get to the airport, Li You can take the subway first, then a bus.

6 _____ Li You finally agrees to go to the airport in Wang Peng's car.

B Listen to the Workbook Dialogue audio, then mark these statements true or false. INTERPRETIVE

1 _____ The woman decides to go home for winter break.

2 _____ The man invites the woman to visit his home.

3 _____ The man and the woman will drive to the man's home together.

4 _____ Plane tickets are not expensive.

Pinyin and Tone

A Identify the characters with the same finals (either *u* or *ü*) and write them in *pinyin*.

路　女　绿　租　录　出　去

1 *u:* _____

2 *ü:* _____

Compare the tones of these characters. Indicate the tones with 1 (first tone), 2 (second tone), 3 (third tone), 4 (fourth tone), or 0 (neutral tone).

1 公 _____ 共 _____   4 先 _____ 线 _____

2 者 _____ 这 _____   5 烦 _____ 饭 _____

3 麻 _____ 妈 _____   6 汽 _____ 起 _____

Speaking

A Answer these questions in Chinese based on the Textbook Dialogue. PRESENTATIONAL

1 What is Li You going to do for winter vacation?

2 What are the two modes of transportation that Li You first considers?

3 Why does Li You abandon her first two choices?

4 How does Li You get to the airport in the end?

B In pairs, find out what your partner plans to do for winter break, and what mode of transportation he/she will use. INTERPERSONAL

C Ask your partner the best way to get to the airport from his/her home, and if there are any alternate routes. INTERPERSONAL

Reading Comprehension

A Read this note, then mark the statements true or false. INTERPRETIVE

小李：

明天是我的生日，你明天到我家来吃晚饭，怎么样？到我家来你可以坐四路公共汽车，也可以坐地铁，都很方便。坐公共汽车慢，可是不用换车。坐地铁快，但是得换车，先坐红线，坐三站，然后换蓝线，坐两站下车就到了。希望你能来！明天见。

小白

十二月五日下午三点

1 _____ Little Li wants to take Little Bai out to dinner tomorrow.

2 _____ To get to Little Bai's home, it is faster to take the subway than the bus.

3 _____ Little Bai's home is not on a bus route or a subway line.

4 _____ Little Bai's birthday is December 5.

5 _____ Little Bai does not expect her friend to drive tomorrow.

B Read this email, then mark the statements true or false. INTERPRETIVE

小白，你好。我是小高。我昨天才知道你这个周末要去机场。你告诉王朋了，可是怎么没告诉我呢？你别坐公共汽车去机场。坐公共汽车不方便，也很慢。你得坐五站，还要换地铁，太麻烦了。我可以开车送你到机场去。我开车开得很好。你今天回宿舍以后给我打个电话，好吗？要是你的飞机票已经买了，我想知道你的飞机是几点的。好，我等你的电话，再见。

1 _____ Little Bai will go to the airport today.

2 _____ Wang Peng knows that Little Bai is going to the airport.

3 _____ According to Little Gao, public transportation to the airport is not convenient.

4 _____ Little Gao considers himself a good driver.

5 _____ Little Gao asks Little Bai to wait for his phone call later today.

6 _____ Little Gao knows that Little Bai has already purchased her plane ticket.

C What tickets are sold here? INTERPRETIVE

_____

_____

Writing and Grammar

A Write the *pinyin* for the characters in the top row, compare them with the *pinyin* of the characters below, then consider the relationship between each pair.

1 机 _____ 2 漂 _____ 3 站 _____ 4 红 _____

几 *(jǐ)* 票 *(piào)* 占 *(zhàn)* 工 *(gōng)*

B Complete these exchanges by creating topic-comment sentences, following the example below.
PRESENTATIONAL

Student A: 我昨天看了一个外国电影。 (I saw that movie, too.)

Student B: 那个电影我也看了。

1 Student A: 你做功课了没有? (Yes.)

Student B: _____

2 Student A: 你喜欢不喜欢喝中国茶? (Yes.)

Student B: _____

3 Student A: 老师给了他一枝笔。 (He gave that pen to his friend.)

Student B: _____

4 Student A: 我昨天去买了一双鞋。 (I don't like that pair.)

Student B: _____

5 Student A: 我今天认识了一个男孩子。 (We all know that boy.)

Student B: _____

Fill in the blanks with 或者 or 还是. PRESENTATIONAL

1 老师正在开会_____给学生考试?

2 你觉得坐地铁方便_____坐公共汽车方便?

3 你想买蓝色的，黑色的，_____咖啡色的裤子?

4 今天晚上我想练习发音_____复习语法。

5 我想要一杯咖啡_____一瓶可乐。

D Based on the images, answer the questions using 先···再····. Follow the example below.
PRESENTATIONAL

Q: 李友今天上什么课?

A: 她今天先上中文课，再上电脑课。

1 Q: 王朋周末想怎么玩儿?

A: _____

2 Q: 张老师明天得做什么?

A: _____

3 Q: 白英爱寒假怎么回家?

A: _____

E Make suggestions by using 还是⋯吧, following the example below. PRESENTATIONAL

Student A: 今天晚上没事儿，我们看电视，好吗？
（没意思，去跳舞）

Student B: 看电视没意思，我们还是去跳舞吧！

1 Student A: 这件黑色的衬衫很便宜。我想买。
（样子不好，别买）

Student B: _____

2 Student A: 我想坐公共汽车去机场。
（太麻烦，打车）

Student B: _____

3 Student A: 我们今天晚上去听音乐会，怎么样？
（没空，明天晚上）

Student B: _____

F Translate these sentences into Chinese. Use the topic-comment sentence structure to translate the bolded text. PRESENTATIONAL

1 Student A: How are we going to get to the airport? By taxi or subway?

_____

Student B: Taxi or subway are both okay.

_____

2 Student A: Give me a ride to school tomorrow, OK?

_____

Student B: Sorry, I'm very busy tomorrow. You'd better take the bus.

_____

3 Student A: I'm flying home this winter break.

_____

Student B: Did you get **the ticket**?

_____

Student A: I got **the ticket** already. It's (a ticket) for December 15.

_____

Student B: On that day, we will have dinner first, and then I'll give you a ride to the airport.

_____

Student A: Really? That would be great. Thank you.

_____

Student B: Don't mention it.

_____

G Little Wang is taking the subway to the airport. Based on the images, describe how he plans to get there from school. PRESENTATIONAL

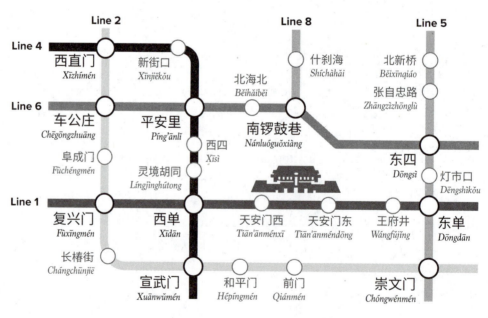

H It's Little Wang's first time taking the Beijing subway. Little Wang is now at Xizhimen (西直门) station. He has to go to Wangfujing (王府井) to do some shopping. Give him detailed directions based on this subway map (note that Line 4 is 四号线). You can write the names of the stations in _pinyin_. PRESENTATIONAL

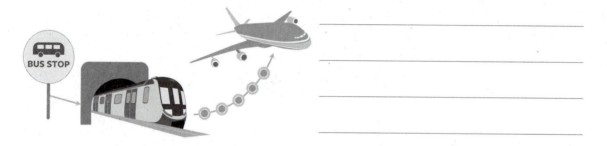

Email: Thanks for the Ride

Listening Comprehension

A Listen to the Textbook Email audio, then mark these statements true or false. INTERPRETIVE

1 _____ Wang Peng gives Li You a ride to the airport.

2 _____ Li You cannot drive.

3 _____ Li You's hometown has buses but no subway.

4 _____ Li You has been busy visiting old friends.

5 _____ Li You feels that everybody drives too slowly.

6 _____ Li You is looking forward to hearing from Wang Peng.

B Listen to the Workbook Dialogue 1 audio, then mark these statements true or false. INTERPRETIVE

1 _____ The woman knows how to get to the man's home.

2 _____ To get to the man's home by subway, first take the Green Line, then change to the Blue Line.

3 _____ The woman needs to take three different buses to get to the man's house.

4 _____ The woman decides to take the bus to the man's place.

C Listen to the Workbook Dialogue 2 audio, then mark these statements true or false. INTERPRETIVE

1 _____ The man will be busy tomorrow.

2 _____ The man claims to be a very good driver.

3 _____ The man will go to the airport with the woman.

4 _____ The woman does not have total confidence in the man.

Pinyin and Tone

A Identify the characters with the same initials (either *j* or *zh*) and write them in *pinyin*.

张　机　紧　假　站　件　者　己

1 *j:* _____

2 *zh:* _____

B Compare the tones of these characters. Indicate the tones with 1 (first tone), 2 (second tone), 3 (third tone), 4 (fourth tone), or 0 (neutral tone).

1 意 _____ 已 _____   5 高 _____ 告 _____

2 花 _____ 话 _____   6 自 _____ 子 _____

3 速 _____ 诉 _____   7 己 _____ 机 _____

4 手 _____ 售 _____   8 每 _____ 妹 _____

Speaking

A Answer these questions based on the Textbook Email. PRESENTATIONAL

1 How do you express New Year greetings in Chinese?

2 Why does Li You thank Wang Peng?

3 What has Li You been doing the past few days?

4 Is Li You a good driver? Explain.

B In pairs, role-play calling and thanking your friend for driving you to the airport. Describe what you've been doing since you returned home, and wish your friend a happy New Year. INTERPERSONAL

C Explain how to get to the airport from your friend's house by referring to the image below. PRESENTATIONAL

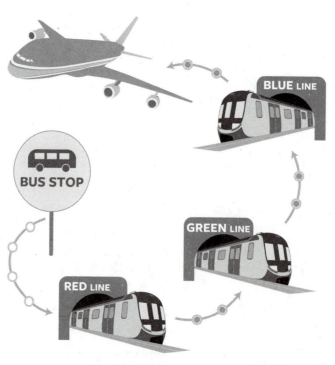

A Read this diary entry, then mark the statements true or false. INTERPRETIVE

小李的一篇日记

今天我开车去小张家找他玩儿。高速公路上的汽车很多，都开得很快。我不知道小张家怎么走，就看手机上的地图。因为在高速公路上开车让我很紧张，所以我开车开得特别慢，很晚才到小张家。

1 ＿＿＿ Little Li visited Little Zhang because they wanted to study together.

2 ＿＿＿ Little Li is a skilled highway driver.

3 ＿＿＿ Little Li had no difficulties finding Little Zhang's place.

4 ＿＿＿ Little Li was probably grateful that she had her cell phone with her.

5 ＿＿＿ Little Li got to Little Zhang's place late because her car is old.

B Read this passage, then mark the statements true or false. INTERPRETIVE

弟弟今天开车送妈妈去机场。高速公路上汽车很多，开得都很快，弟弟很紧张，所以开得特别慢。妈妈的飞机是两点半的，他们三点才到机场。机场的人告诉妈妈，她只能坐明天的飞机了。弟弟很不好意思，说明天再开车送妈妈去机场。可是妈妈说她明天还是自己坐出租汽车吧。

1 ＿＿＿ My brother is a very experienced driver.

2 ＿＿＿ The traffic on the highway was light, so people drove fast.

3 ＿＿＿ My brother drove very slowly because he was nervous.

4 ＿＿＿ When my brother and mother arrived at the airport, her flight had departed.

5 ＿＿＿ There were later flights today, but my mother preferred to wait until tomorrow.

6 ＿＿＿ My mother will most likely not ride in the same car to the airport tomorrow.

Read this passage, then answer the questions in English. INTERPRETIVE

在中国，小孩都特别喜欢中国新年，因为他们可以穿新衣，穿新鞋，爸爸妈妈也给他们钱。不过，李小红告诉我她不喜欢中国新年。她三十岁，有先生，可是没有孩子，所以别人不给她钱，她得给别人的小孩很多钱。李小红还说新年的时候公共汽车很少，她自己也没有车，所以出去玩也不方便。她觉得中国新年太没意思了。

1 Which two Chinese New Year traditions make children happy? Explain in detail.

_____

2 Which two Chinese New Year traditions make Li Xiaohong unhappy? Explain in detail.

_____

3 Is Li Xiaohong male or female? How do you know?

_____

D The following are directions to a theme park. Identify at least three means of transportation that tourists can use to get there. INTERPRETIVE

自行开车

花莲县寿丰乡台11线10公里处。

飞　机

台北　远东、复兴航空公司，
航程约35分钟。

台中　华信航空公司，航程约1小时。

高雄　远东、华信航空公司，
航程约50分钟。

铁　路

台北　观光列车由台北专车直达
花莲新站，约需3小时半。

台中　经由台北转由北回铁路直达。

高雄　经南回铁路由东部干线北上抵达。

公　路

大有巴士客运专车直达花莲市区后，
转搭花莲客运往台东、丰滨方向。

市区公车

花莲旧火车站发车往台东方向经海岸线。

_____

_____

Writing and Grammar

A Write the common radical and the characters, then provide their meanings in English. Consider their relationship with the radical.

送 速 这 近 道 边

1. ⊞ _____

2. ⊞ _____

3. ⊞ _____

4. ⊞ _____

5. ⊞ _____

6. ⊞ _____

7. ⊞ _____

B Based on the images, describe what makes Li You nervous. PRESENTATIONAL

什么让李友紧张?

1. _____

2. _____

3. _____

C | Answer these questions according to your own circumstances. INTERPERSONAL

1 什么让你紧张？

_____

2 什么让你高兴？

_____

3 什么让你不好意思？

_____

D | Answer these questions with 每⋯都⋯, following the example below. PRESENTATIONAL

Q: 他<u>晚上</u>看电视吗？

A: 他每天晚上都看电视。

1 Q: 她<u>早上</u>走高速公路吗？

A: _____

2 Q: 考试的时候<u>哪一个学生</u>很紧张？

A: _____

3 Q: 常老师<u>哪个周末</u>回家？

A: _____

4 Q: 那个商店的<u>什么衣服</u>很贵？

A: _____

E | Translate these sentences into Chinese. PRESENTATIONAL

1 Student A: You speak Chinese so well. How do you normally prepare for your Chinese class?

_____

_____

Student B: I listen to the audio every morning.

_____

2 Student A: We'll have dinner first, then we'll go dancing. My treat!

_____

Student B: I feel bad about making you spend money.

_____

3 Student A: I'll give you a ride to school today.

_____

Student B: Never mind. I'd better take the bus.

_____

Student A: Why?

_____

Student B: You drive too fast, and it makes me nervous.

_____

Student A: Is that so?

_____

4 Student A: I like New York. This city is so interesting.

_____

Student B: I also think New York is quite nice. Its subway is especially convenient.

_____

5 Student A: Do you know how to send text messages in Chinese?

_____

Student B: Yes. I send messages in Chinese to my Chinese friends.

_____

Student A: Really? Cool.

_____

Student B: Everybody knows how. I'll teach you.

_____

Student A: Great! New Year is coming. I want to message my friends and wish them a happy New Year.

_____

_____

Student B: OK, I'll teach you now.

_____

F Comment on your city and highway driving skills. If you don't drive, comment on people's driving habits in your city or its public transportation system. PRESENTATIONAL

_____

_____

_____

_____

G The holiday season is approaching. Email or send a text message to your friends in Chinese. Ask them how they are doing and wish them a happy New Year. PRESENTATIONAL

_____

_____

_____

_____

Bringing It Together (Lessons 6–10)

A Compare the characters' pronunciation and tones, then write them in *pinyin*.

1 喜欢 _____   希望 _____

2 告诉 _____   高速 _____

3 听录音 _____   换绿线 _____

4 多少钱 _____   都是钱 _____

5 售货员 _____   或者 _____

Radicals

A Group these characters according to their radicals.

客　得　笔　慢　错　然　词　线　贵

衫　钱　澡　等　室　货　烦　宿　绿

让　很　练　紧　语　懂　衬　律　笑

员　第　铁　裤　汽　念　照　洗　试

Radical　　　Characters

1 _____ _____

2 _____ _____

3 _____ _____

4 _____ _____

5 _____ _____

6 _____ _____

7 _____ _____

8 _____ _____

9 _____ _____

10 _____ _____

11 _____ _____

VO Compounds

A Circle the verbs that are VO compounds.

学习　　　知道　　　开会　　　写字

告诉　　　付钱　　　坐地铁　　下车

说话　　　预习

Communication

A Ask your classmates the following questions about school life. Jot down their answers, then report to the class on who has the most in common with you.

1 你是大学几年级的学生?

_____

2 你的专业是什么? _____

3 你这个学期上什么课？

_____

4 你每天有几节课？ _____

5 你最喜欢上什么课？

_____

6 你最不喜欢上什么课？

_____

7 你的考试多不多？ _____

8 你什么课考试考得最好？

_____

B In pairs, ask and answer the following questions about studying Chinese. Present an oral or written report to your class based on the information you collect.

1 你为什么学中文？

_____

2 你觉得学中文有意思吗？

_____

3 你常常跟谁一起练习说中文？

_____

4 你去老师的办公室问问题吗？

_____

5 你觉得每课的生词多不多？语法难不难？

_____

6 你平常先听录音再练习汉字还是先练习汉字再听录音?

_____

7 你平常上新课以前预习吗?

_____

8 你平常考试以前找谁帮你复习?

_____

9 你平常考试考得怎么样?

_____

10 你觉得你的老师说话说得快不快?

_____

11 你觉得你写汉字写得怎么样?

_____

12 你会不会用中文发短信、写信、写日记或者写电子邮件?

_____

C Ask your friend the following questions to find the perfect birthday gift.

1 你希望有件新衬衫,有条新裤子,还是有双新鞋?

_____

2 你（不）喜欢什么颜色？

_____

3 衬衫你穿多大的？ _____

4 裤子你穿几号的？鞋呢？

_____

5 你希望我自己去买，还是你跟我一起去买？

_____

6 要是大小、长短不合适，你希望我帮你去
商店换，还是你自己去换？

_____

_____

D Before getting in a car with your friend, ask him/her the following questions.

1 你会开车吗？ _____

2 要是你昨天晚上没睡觉，你能开车吗？

_____

3 你的车新不新？ _____

4 你开车开得怎么样？ _____

5 你常常一边开车，一边打手机吗？

_____

6 你在高速公路上开车紧张不紧张？

_____

7 要是你的车有问题，我们坐公共汽车还是打车？

_____